The Hubris Syndrome

Bush, Blair and the Intoxication of Power

David Owen

METHUEN

First published in Great Britain in 2007
This revised edition published in 2012 by
Methuen & Co
35 Hospital Fields Road
York YO10 4DZ

A CIP catalogue record for this book is available from the British
Library.

ISBN 978-0-413-77727-0

Typeset by SX Composing DTP, Rayleigh, Essex
Printed and bound by CPI Group (UK) Ltd, Croydon, CR0 4YY

Contents

Introduction

I had no intention of producing a revised version of *The Hubris Syndrome* published five years ago in 2007 until the Report of the Inquiry into the War in Iraq, established in 2009, reported. But as this Report was repeatedly delayed I decided, with nearly six months to run until it was expected to be published in 2012, it would be worth republishing now. Hubris Syndrome has been refined and with articles about it as in *Brain* and *The Psychiatrist* referred to in the book, is much closer to professional acceptance. This book is about personality change, not primarily about the Iraq War. New material on Tony Blair's decision making and personality has been revealed in evidence to the Iraq Inquiry. I have also gleaned much new information over the past five years on Bush and Blair through memoirs written by all the key players in the US and UK on the Iraq war. There has also been the strange and quite unprecedented event of a fictional play *Loyalty* published by Oberon Press. The interest in the play stems from it having been written as a fictionalized memoir by Sarah Helm, who at the time was the partner of, and is now married to, Jonathan Powell, the Chief of Staff to Prime Minister Tony Blair throughout his period in office. It was performed in London in July 2011 at the Hampstead Theatre. It focused on the lead up to the Iraq war in March 2003, its aftermath in September 2003 and in September 2004.

Sir John Chilcot, the Chairman of the Inquiry, went to see the play, and according to a headline in the *Observer* on Sunday, 16 October 2011 "Chilcot reconsiders findings after attending play on build-up to war". Apparently after thinking about what he had heard in the theatre, he was determined to discover whether there was any truth behind the fictional play. Presumably whether there was fact not just fiction in the undisclosed conversation between Bush and Blair on or around 4 March 2003 preceded by a one-on-one meeting of Blair with the head of MI6. Also whether what was discussed was new, but later shown to be incorrect intelligence which pushed Blair over his threshold for agreeing formally that the UK island in the Indian Ocean, Diego Garcia, could be used by American planes, something for which Donald Rumsfeld was pushing hard. Chilcot would have been strengthened in any feeling that the Inquiry might not have been told the full story if he had also read the extraordinarily frank foreword by Sir Sherard Cowper-Coles to the published edition of the play. Cowper-Coles had been our Ambassador in Tel Aviv at the time of the Iraq war and had seen the most secret intelligence coming in to the Embassy in sealed plastic envelopes suggesting that Saddam Hussein had WMD. He later went on to serve in the key role of UK Ambassador in Afghanistan. He wrote:

"As Sarah Helm's play reminds us so painfully, what

compounded the agony of the initial catastrophic error was the discovery not only that Saddam had no weapons of mass destruction (as Robin Cook had warned the House of Commons on the eve of invasion) but that the intelligence suggesting he had such weapons was false or fabricated."

"Naturally the details of the play's plot are fiction, and have to be, not least for legal reasons. But that should not obscure the deeper truths about deceit, both wilful and wishful, at the highest levels of government which the play sets out, so graphically."

Sir John Chilcot, and fellow members of the Inquiry, were by the summer of 2011, when the Report was initially expected to be published, and when he must have seen the play, apparently locked in a dispute with Whitehall about what documents could be released for their final Report. In particular they appear to have been determined to publish extracts of written messages and accounts of telephone conversations between Prime Minister Blair and President George W Bush. It is vital that they win this argument with Whitehall about publishing extracts before the report is finalised. Under the existing rules in the UK and the US, both Blair and Bush have been able to quote from their letters in their memoirs. In the UK, Alastair Campbell and Jonathan Powell, both at the time of the War, civil servants, have been allowed to make references to the Blair-Bush exchanges. In the case of Campbell, in evidence to the Inquiry, he described the letters as "very frank . . ." The tenor of them was that . . . "we are absolutely with you in making [Saddam Hussein] face up to his obligations. But if that can't be done diplomatically, if it has to be done militarily, then Britain will be there." As Sir John has already written the Whitehall argumentation "leads to the position that individuals may disclose privileged information (without sanction) whilst a committee of privy councillors established by a former Prime Minister to review the issues, cannot". It is essential in the public interest that on this the Inquiry's position is upheld.

As a consequence of this dispute, and possibly also the play, instead of the Report coming out before Christmas 2011, it is now postponed until at least the summer of 2012. We will see then whether the Inquiry triumph over Whitehall and whether the delay had anything to do with the play *Loyalty*. It looks likely that the play will be shown to have been at least the catalyst for a more stringent review of what some of the key figures in No. 10's conduct of the Iraq war may have omitted to say in their initial evidence. I profoundly hope the Report will not be yet another example of a "Whitehall whitewash".

Many people have helped in discussion and debate on the original paperback book published in 2007 and now in its substantively revised version in 2012. To all of them I offer my personal thanks. This version covers much new ground on events in Iraq drawing on much new material in the memoirs of President Bush and Prime Minister Blair written in 2010, Vice-President Dick Cheney, and Defense Secretary Donald Rumsfeld, written in 2011 and Secretary Condoleezza Rice in 2011. It also draws on the wealth of evidence submitted to, and already published by, the Iraq Inquiry up until September 2011. I hope it will help people decide whether the final report of the Inquiry fulfils its responsibilities. The Inquiry chaired by Sir John Chilcot was established, after much Parliamentary pres - sure, in June 2009 by the then Prime Minister, Gordon Brown. The book also reflects much of the new writing and research into hubris syndrome that followed the initial publication of this book.

John Wakefield, whom I have known since the late 1970s and with whom I have campaigned politically against the euro, deserves very special mention. With surgical precision, he cut and made suggestions for my initial manuscript and in doing so, greatly improved it.

Doctors of medicine, including my son Gareth, at the Institute of Psychiatry, King's College London, have been an immense help, as has Argyris Stringaris, also at the Institute. I have been fortunate to have had the advice of Paul Flynn, a metabolic physician at the University of Cambridge; Dr Kevin Cahill, Professor in Tropical Medicine and Director of the Center for International Health and Cooperation in New York; Professor Gabriel Kune, Emeritus Professor of Surgery, University of Melbourne; Dr David Ward, consultant cardiologist, St George's Hospital, London; Professor Anne Curtis, Yale University and Professor Jonathan Davidson of Duke University with whom I wrote an article in *Brain* in 2009.

I am grateful to the following libraries that have gone out of their way to help. First, and foremost, the House of Lords

Library; the Library of the University of Birmingham, and the Library of the University of Liverpool, where I was Chancellor, and where all my personal archives are held.

My profound thanks to my publishers, Methuen, and in particular Jonathan Wadman. Also Alan Gordon Walker, who suggested separating *The Hubris Syndrome* from a much longer book, *In Sickness and In Power: Illness in Heads of Government during the last 100 years*, originally published in 2008 and with a revised paperback edition in 2011.

The Pulitzer Prize-winning historian Barbara Tuchman wrote about power in *The March of Folly: From Troy to Vietnam*:

"We are less aware that it breeds folly; that the power to command frequently causes failure to think; that the responsibility of power often fades as its exercise augments. The overall responsibility of power is to govern as reasonably as possible in the interest of the state and its citizens. A duty in that process is to keep well-informed, to heed information, to keep mind and judgement open and to resist the insidious spell of wooden-headedness. If the mind is open enough to perceive that a given policy is harming rather than serving self-interest, and self-confident enough to acknowledge it, and wise enough to reverse it, that is a summit in the art of government."

Prologue: The intoxication of power

The sicknesses which heads of government have either brought to office or developed while occupying high office, and the consequences of being ill for the business of government, are a fascinating study.[1] But there is another interesting and far from uncommon phenomenon to which all leaders are susceptible, particularly politicians: how, with many of them, the very experience of holding office seems to develop into something that causes them to behave in ways which, on the face of it at least, seem symptomatic of a change in personality. It is a phenomenon captured in popular phrases such as 'power has gone to his head', 'he's taken leave of his senses', 'she's off her trolley', 'he's lost his marbles' or 'she's lost all touch with reality'. Emotive language is best avoided by the medical profession, which rightly eschews even expressions such as 'madness' and 'lunacy' when talking about mental health. But the phenomenon of something happening to a person's mental stability when in power has been observed for centuries and the causal link between holding power and aberrant behaviour that was captured by Bertrand Russell who drew attention to factual truth and humility being sacrificed as part of an intoxication:

The concept of 'truth' as something dependent upon facts largely outside human control has been one of the ways in which philosophy hitherto has inculcated the necessary element of humility. When this check upon pride is removed, a further step is taken on the road towards a certain kind of madness – the intoxication of power.[2]

Power is a heady drug which not every political leader has the necessary rooted character to counteract: to do so requires a combination of common sense, humour, decency, scepticism and even cynicism that treats power for what it is – a privileged opportunity to influence, and sometimes to determine, the turn of events.

Perhaps the most profound, though non-medical, study of this was made in the ancient world. The Greeks developed the notion of *hubris* to characterise and explore it. The most basic meaning was simply as a description of an act: a hubristic act was one in which a powerful figure, puffed up with overweening pride and self-confidence, treated others with insolence and contempt. They seemed to get kicks from using their power to treat others in this way, but such dishonouring behaviour was strongly condemned in ancient Greece. In a famous passage from Plato's *Phaedrus*, a predisposition to hubris is defined: 'But when desire irrationally drags us toward pleasures and rules within us, its rule is called excess [*hubris*].'[3] Plato saw this 'rule of desire' as something irrational that drags people into doing the wrong thing through acts of hubris. In his *Rhetoric*, Aristotle picks up the element of desire Plato identifies in hubris and argues that the pleasure someone seeks from an act of hubris lies in showing himself as superior. 'That is why the young and the wealthy are given to insults [*hubristai*, i.e. being hubristic]; for they think that, in committing them [acts of hubris], they are showing superiority.' [4]

But it was in drama rather than philosophy that the notion was developed further to explore the patterns of hubristic behaviour, its causes and consequences. A hubristic career proceeded along something like the following course. The hero wins glory and acclamation by achieving unwonted success against the odds. The experience then goes to the hero's head: he begins to treat others, mere ordinary mortals, with contempt and disdain and develops such confidence in his own ability that he begins to think himself capable of anything. This excessive self-confidence leads him into misinterpreting the reality around him and into making mistakes. Eventually he gets his come-uppance and meets his nemesis, which destroys him.

Nemesis is the name of the goddess of retribution, and often in Greek drama the gods arrange nemesis because a hubristic act is seen as one in which the perpetrator tries to defy the reality ordained by them. The hero committing the hubristic act seeks to transgress the human condition, imagining himself to be superior and to have powers more like those of the gods. But the gods will have none of that: so it is they who destroy him. The moral is that we should beware of allowing power and success to go to our heads.

The theme of hubris has fascinated playwrights, no doubt because it provides the opportunity to explore human character within highly dramatic action. Shakespeare's *Coriolanus* is a study in it. But the pattern of the hubristic career is one that will immediately strike a chord in anyone who has studied the history of political leaders. The hubristic posture has been described by the philosopher David E. Cooper as 'excessive self-confidence, an "up yours!" attitude to authority, pre-emptive dismissal of warnings and advice, taking oneself as a model.'[5] Another philosopher, Hannah Arendt, who admired ancient Athens, has written about the shortcomings of its ruler Pericles, who was possessed by 'the hubris of power', and has compared him unfavourably with Solon, the law maker of Athens.[6] The historian Ian Kershaw aptly titled the two volumes of his biography of Hitler *Hubris* and *Nemesis*.[7]

Hubris is almost an occupational hazard for leading politicians, as it is for leaders in other fields, such as the military and business, for it feeds on the isolation that often builds up around such leaders. At one point, I was accused of megalomania.[8] A study of General Motors described business leaders who deceive themselves and distance themselves from reality. It argued that a point often comes when such individuals are no longer living in the same world as the organisation they lead, and it ended by describing the horror that arises from the claims of powerful mortals to be more than mortal. 'The Greeks called this hubris and they knew that the gods, whom we might refer to as reality, do not stand for it. They demand humility.'[9]

The havoc which hubristic heads of government can wreak is usually suffered by the people in whose name they govern. The virtues of a representative democracy lie in the scope it gives elected leaders to exercise real leadership and to show the decisiveness most voters prefer to hesitation, doubt and vacillation. But the exercise of that leadership needs to carry the trust of the electorate, which is usually lost when the leader crosses the borderline between decisive and hubristic leadership. What interests me is whether that borderline, marked as yet only by loose phrases, can be defined more precisely and whether philosophers, the medical profession, psychologists and anthropologists could assist in defining it.

Medicine's approach to mental ill health often has to be conducted in the absence of any physical symptoms or disease markers: what alerts the medical practitioner to a problem is not a physical symptom but aberrant behaviour of some sort. Very often the medical profession may be unable to discover any cause of this behaviour but will nonetheless regard it as constituting mental ill health. Certain patterns of such behaviour are often categorised as symptomatic of specific syndromes. Studies are needed on the behaviour of leaders in all walks of life to see whether there might be an identifiable syndrome at work. If identified, it might be easier to predict, prevent and even perhaps treat through mentoring or other techniques.

In adopting this approach, of categorising specific patterns of behaviour as symptomatic of defined syndromes, the medical profession is not so much *discovering* disease, as it might be said to have done in a straightforward sense when it discovered, say, tuberculosis, as *deciding* that certain patterns of behaviour constitute a change in personality. This is a very important distinction because it highlights two quite different but equally valid practices for establishing what should and should not be recognised as illness. In agreeing to the existence of a particular syndrome, or clinical picture, the medical profession is not bowing to the unrefuted, objective evidence derived from experiment, as when some diseases are discovered, but is taking a collective, pragmatic *decision* that it is sensible to deem a certain pattern of behavioural symptoms, more often found together than separately, as amounting to a syndrome. A good example of this is post-traumatic stress disorder. Here the condition cannot occur unless there has been a traumatic event. It is characterised by a set of signs and symptoms, such as flashbacks, hypervigilance and nightmares around the event, and now after much debate and controversy it is recognised as a syndrome which is acquired.

I have been exploring the hypothesis that there is a pattern of hubristic behaviour manifest in some leaders, particularly political leaders, which could legitimately be deemed to constitute a medically recognised syndrome, which I have called hubris syndrome. In April 2011 *The Psychiatrist* published a detailed assessment of my writing by a former Dean of the Institute of Psychiatry and someone who identified the syndrome bulimia.[10] Hubris is not an easy diagnosis to make for the individual affected can appear completely normal in their social life; even those in close contact with their decision-making may not pick up, in the early stages, a change of behaviour. Some psychiatrists believe that hubristic behaviour is systemic, a product of the environment in which the leader operates. On the other hand this hubristic build-up gives the impression that it has become self-generating, that an individual is gripped by something which is no longer driven by outside factors but comes from within that individual. It is this element which comprises hubris syndrome.

In an article in *Brain* in 2009, "Hubris Syndrome: An Acquired Personality Disorder?" Jonathan Davidson, a professor of psychiatry at Duke University, and I also drew attention to the neurobiology of hubris syndrome. We mentioned one study that had identified frontostriatal and limbic-striatal dopaminergic pathways in the brain as important regulators of impulsive and/or rigid behaviours.[11] There have been many other interesting findings in the area of neuroscience since that article. But one recent study in 2010 is, I think, worth highlighting. It showed that, in 35 patients with Parkinson's disease, an individual's strength of belief in their being likely to improve can of itself directly modulate brain dopamine release.[12] What they call conscious expectation in this randomised study describes the probability the individual is given that they will be receiving active medication with levodopa. Amongst those who were actually given a placebo and a 75% probability of it being active medication there was significant endogenous dopamine release in the ventral striatum. No such release occurred with the lesser probability of 25% or 50%. What we need now are more studies on brain dopamine levels in decision makers. The neuro-biological effects of conscious expectation in this experimental context may be similar to the conscious expectations which go along with the intoxication of power in hubris syndrome.

We need, on a multidisciplinary basis, to use all the necessary skills. Hubris syndrome is not confined just to politicians. It is vital to assess the role of personality change in leaders of the 2008 financial crisis. A number of us have just established a research charity called the Daedalus Trust[13] to raise money for such research. We chose the name Daedalus, from Greek mythology because he flew with the waxed wings he had designed but had the good sense to warn his son Icarus of the dangers of flying high, too close to the sun, and flying low, too close to the waves. He was a risk taker, an entrepreneur, which society needs, but he was also wise and understood the limits of his ambition. The complexity and necessity of risk taking needs studying, not in a hostile and regulation driven way but in a spirit of understanding. There are positives as well as negatives surrounding hubristic leadership, particularly in business.

At British Petroleum a brilliant and initially very successful former Chief Executive, John Browne, began to demonstrate many of the contemptuous features of hubris syndrome in his private life and this may have led to a corporate hubris at BP that extended well beyond his tenure of office.[14] At Royal Bank of Scotland, RBS, the Chief Executive Fred Goodwin also appeared to have signs of hubris syndrome, something that needs deep study. At Halifax Bank of Scotland, HBOS, both the Chairman and the Chief Executive appeared to have been unable to rein in a very senior corporate executive and that needs studying.

Identifying hubristic leaders and hubristic cultures and containing them presents, therefore, an immense challenge. Such leaders are often, when first appointed, well qualified and experienced and have not given any warning signs to their electors, in the case of politicians, or Boards of Directors, in the case of bankers and industrialists, that they could develop hubris syndrome. By definition I do not use the term hubris syndrome where there is known history of psychiatric illness or of long-standing behavioural problems. Such people may be very hubristic but it seemed better to respect their medical diagnosis while recognising such disease may all be part of a spectrum of personality that can change and develop in power into a different personality. It is in all our interests that we learn more about such people, their hubristic cultures and develop informal systems of peer review if we are to prevent the making of damaging decisions in the future.

The hubris syndrome

The behavioural symptoms in a head of government which might trigger the diagnosis of hubris syndrome typically grow in strength and are represented by more than three or four symptoms from the following tentative list, before any such diagnosis could be contemplated:

- a narcissistic propensity to see the world primarily as an arena in which they can exercise power and seek glory rather than as a place with problems that need approaching in a pragmatic and non-self-referential manner;
- a predisposition to take actions which seem likely to cast them in a good light – i.e. in order to enhance their image;
- a disproportionate concern with image and presentation;
- a messianic manner of talking about what they are doing and a tendency to exaltation;
- an identification of themselves with the state to the extent that they regard the outlook and interests of the two as identical;
- a tendency to talk of themselves in the third person or using the royal 'we';

- excessive confidence in their own judgement and contempt for the advice or criticism of others;
- exaggerated self-belief, bordering on a sense of omnipotence, in what they personally can achieve;
- a belief that rather than being accountable to the mundane court of colleagues or public opinion, the real court to which they answer is much greater: History or God;
- an unshakeable belief that in that court they will be vindicated;
- restlessness, recklessness and impulsiveness;
- loss of contact with reality; often associated with progressive isolation;
- a tendency to allow their 'broad vision', especially their conviction about the moral rectitude of a proposed course of action, to obviate the need to consider other aspects of it, such as its practicality, cost and the possibility of unwanted outcomes;
- a consequent type of incompetence in carrying out a policy, which could be called hubristic incompetence. This is where things go wrong precisely because too much self-confidence has led the leader not to bother worrying about the nuts and bolts of a policy. It can be allied to an incurious nature. It is to be distinguished from ordinary incompetence, where the necessary detailed work on the complex issues involved completed but mistakes in decision-making are made nonetheless.

Most syndromes of personality tend to manifest themselves in people by the age of eighteen and stay with them for the rest of their lives. Hubris syndrome is different in that it might be an acquired personality disorder, something which manifests itself in leaders only when in power – and usually only after they have been wielding power for some time – and which then may well abate once power is lost. In that sense it is a syndrome of position as much as of the person and can manifest at any age. And the circumstances in which the position is held clearly affect the likelihood that a leader will succumb to it. The key external factors would seem to be these: holding substantial power; minimal constraint on the leaders exercising such personal authority; and the length of time they stay in power.

In this regard, for those who have a medical background, it follows a tradition which acknowledges the existence of pathological personality change, such as the four types in ICD-10: enduring personality change after trauma, psychiatric illness, chronic pain or unspecified type (ICD-10, 1994). However in developing the acquired argument further in the article in *Brain* in 2009, Professor Davidson and I mapped the broad affinities of hubris syndrome with the DSM-IV criteria for narcissistic personality disorder, NPD, antisocial personality disorder and histrionic personality disorder. These three personality disorders also appear in ICD-10, although NPD is presented in an appendix as a provisional condition, whose clinical or scientific status is regarded as uncertain. ICD-10 considers NPD to be sufficiently important to warrant more study, but that it is not yet ready for international acceptance. In defining the boundaries, one of the more important questions may be to understand whether hubris syndrome is essentially the same as NPD, a subtype of NPD or a separate condition. As shown in Table 1, seven of the 14 possible defining symptoms are also among the criteria for NPD in DSM-IV, and two correspond to those for antisocial personality and histrionic personality disorders, APD and HPD respectively, (American Psychiatric Association, 2000). The five remaining symptoms are unique, in the sense they have not been classified elsewhere: (5) conflation of self with the nation or organisation; (6) use of the royal "we"; (10) an unshakable belief that a higher court (history or God) will provide vindication; (12) restlessness, recklessness and impulsiveness; and (13) moral rectitude that overrides practicalities, cost and outcome.

In making the diagnosis of hubris syndrome we suggested that 3 of the 14 defining symptoms should be present of which at least one must be amongst the five components identified as unique.

Few people exercise real power in any society and the frequency amongst those 'at risk' is low but the potential importance of the syndrome derives from the extensive damage that can be done by the small number of people who are affected.

Both Jonathan Davidson and I have written elsewhere in detail about the health of heads of government. Partly as a consequence, the examples of hubris we described are drawn

Table 1 The symptoms of hubris syndrome

Proposed criteria for hubris syndrome, and their correspondence to features of cluster B personality disorders in DSM-IV
1. A narcissistic propensity to see their world primarily as an arena in which to exercise power and seek glory; NPD.6
2. A predisposition to take actions which seem likely to cast the individual in a good light—i.e. in order to enhance image; NPD.1
3. A disproportionate concern with image and presentation; NPD.3
4. A messianic manner of talking about current activities and a tendency to exaltation; NPD.2
5. An identification with the nation, or organization to the extent that the individual regards his/her outlook and interests as identical; (unique)
6. A tendency to speak in the third person or use the royal 'we'; (unique)
7. Excessive confidence in the individual's own judgement and contempt for the advice or criticism of others; NPD.9
8. Exaggerated self-belief, bordering on a sense of omnipotence, in what they personally can achieve; NPD.1 and 2 combined
9. A belief that rather than being accountable to the mundane court of colleagues or public opinion, the court to which they answer is: History or God; NPD.3
10. An unshakable belief that in that court they will be vindicated; (unique)
11. Loss of contact with reality; often associated with progressive isolation; APD 3 and 5
12. Restlessness, recklessness and impulsiveness; (unique)
13. A tendency to allow their 'broad vision', about the moral rectitude of a proposed course, to obviate the need to consider practicality, cost or outcomes; (unique)
14. Hubristic incompetence, where things go wrong because too much self-confidence has led the leader not to worry about the nuts and bolts of policy; HPD.5

APD = Anti-Social Personality Disorder; HPD = Histrionic Personality Disorder; NPD = Narcissistic Personality Disorder.

from the US presidents and UK Prime Ministers in office over the last 100 years; but also it is because there are far more extensive biographical sources for heads of governments than for other categories of leader.

Table 2 Hubris syndrome amongst the 18 US Presidents in office since 1908

Presidents	Related illnesses to hubris	Impairment evident to others or sought treatment	Hubristic traits	Hubris syndrome
Theodore Roosevelt 1901–09	Bipolar disorder	Yes	Yes	No
Woodrow Wilson 1913–21	Anxiety disorder Major depressive disorder Personality change due to stroke	Yes	Yes	?
Franklin D. Roosevelt 1933–45	None	No	Yes	No
John F. Kennedy 1961–63	Addison's disease Amphetamine abuse	Yes	Yes	No
Lyndon B. Johnson 1963–69	Bipolar 1 disorder	Yes	Yes	No
Richard Nixon 1969–74	Alcoholic abuse	Yes	Yes	?
George W. Bush 2001–09	History of alcohol-related problems	Yes	Yes	Yes

? uncertain - probable.

Table 3 Hubris syndrome amongst the 26 UK Prime Ministers in office since 1908

Prime Ministers	Related illnesses to hubris	Impairment evident to others Treatment sought	Hubristic traits	Hubris syndrome
Herbert Asquith 1908–16	Alcohol abuse	Yes	Yes	No
David Lloyd George 1916–22	None	Yes	Yes	Yes
Neville Chamberlain 1937–40	None	Yes	Yes	Yes
Winston Churchill 1940–45, 1951–55	Major depressive disorder; cyclothymic features	Yes	Yes	No
Anthony Eden 1955–57	Amphetamine abuse	Yes	Yes	No
Margaret Thatcher 1979–90	None	Yes	Yes	Yes
Tony Blair 1997–2007	None	Yes	Yes	Yes

It would be a great mistake, however, to think that hubris syndrome only develops in politicians. It can appear in anyone who is in a leadership position. It is particularly a problem, as we saw in the global financial crisis from 2008, amongst bankers and financiers. An atmosphere of omnipotence can easily grow around any leader, but political leaders are particularly vulnerable, even democratically elected ones. They are surrounded by deference and hierarchy within government, and the leader's views are often recycled back and alternative views can easily be ignored or dismissed. A bunker mentality can build up around any leader.

Though hubris syndrome may be an acquired syndrome of personality, a leader's susceptibility to it is in part dependent on their own personality, their own character. Two politicians in my lifetime whom I most admire and took power in 1945 clearly had an inner image of themselves which prevented them from being intoxicated by power. US President Harry Truman and the British Prime Minister Clement Attlee, both achieved remarkable and unexpected success but it did not go to their heads. Churchill's famous quip about Attlee – that he was 'a modest man with a good deal to be modest about' – may have been intended as a slur but the modesty he disparaged protected Attlee from succumbing to hubris syndrome.

The medical issue over Churchill is whether he suffered not simply from depression but from manic depression, or what is now called bipolar disorder. I dispute this diagnosis believing there is no case of an incontrovertibly manic episode in his life.

I am also sceptical of attributing examples of his sometimes bizarre behaviour to mania. For instance, some have used his tendency to dictate to a secretary while in the bath – and certainly he was not self-conscious about being in the nude – as diagnostic of mania, but this lack of self-consciousness was quite common in his social class.

Nonetheless, the testimony of those who worked closely with Churchill does imply a manic as well as a depressive side to him. Oliver Harvey, the private secretary to Anthony Eden, then Foreign Secretary, noted in his diary on 13 July 1943: 'The PM [Churchill] was in a crazy state of exultation. The battle has gone to the old man's head. The quantities of liquor he consumed – champagne, brandies, whiskies – were incredible.' [1] What is interesting here is that Harvey says it is the battle, not the alcohol, which has gone to Churchill's head. And interestingly he uses the phrase 'crazy state of exultation', a symptom which psychiatrists would certainly take into account in diagnosing bipolar disorder.

Yet more revealing of the exceptional character of the man is the picture painted by General Hastings Ismay, Churchill's military chief of staff, in a letter written on 3 April 1942 to General Claude Auchinleck, in the desert of north Africa. 'The Auk', as he was called, had recently been on the receiving end of Churchill's volatile mood. Ismay wrote:

You cannot judge the PM by ordinary standards: he is not in the least like anyone that you or I have ever met. He is a mass of contradictions. He is either on the crest of the wave, or in the trough; either highly laudatory, or bitterly condemnatory; either in an angelic temper, or a hell of a rage; when he isn't fast asleep he's a volcano. There are no half-measures in his make-up. He is a child of nature with moods as variable as an April day, and he apparently sees no difference between harsh words spoken to a friend, and forgotten within the hour under the influence of friendly argument, and the same harsh words telegraphed to a friend thousands of miles away – with no opportunity for 'making it up' . . .

I think I can lay claim to having been called every name under the sun during the last six months – except perhaps a coward; but I know perfectly well in the midst of these storms that they mean exactly nothing, and that before the sun goes down, I shall be summoned to an intimate and delightfully friendly talk – to 'make it up'. [2]

Roy Jenkins describes Churchill, in the late spring of 1944, as exhibiting a

great fluctuation of mood, with bursts of energy and indeed brilliance of performance intervening in a general pattern of lassitude and gloom, stemming largely from an awareness that none of his interlocutors – Stalin, Roosevelt, de Gaulle – would do exactly what he wished and a growing feeling of impotence to impose his will. He approached victory with much less buoyancy than he had confronted the menace of defeat four years before. [3]

I have written in detail elsewhere[4] on why I believe, on balance, Churchill had neither bipolar disorder nor hubris syndrome. Churchill undoubtedly suffered from depression but his humour helped prevent him developing hubris syndrome more than any modesty. When one of his very young grandsons interrupted the old man in his study with the question 'Grandfather, is it true that you are the greatest man in the world?', Churchill replied, 'Yes it is. Now bugger off!'

The one period in which there could be some questioning of whether Churchill's mood as Prime Minister might have become manic, certainly swinging to at least hypomania, was in May and June 1940. His daughter, Mary, wrote of this time "he knew the deadly nature of the onslaught which was being proposed just across the Channel and, above all, he knew our nakedness . . ." "He drove himself and he drove others with a flail . . ." "He must have become extremely overbearing and tyrannical to many of those who served him." On 27 June 1940 Clementine, recognising a significant change in her husband's behaviour wrote to him after some hesitation a moving but also a brave and important letter. [5] An extract reads:

10 Downing Street,
Whitehall
June 27, 1940

My Darling,

I hope you will forgive me if I tell you something I feel you ought to know.

One of the men in your entourage (a devoted friend) has been to me & told me that there is a danger of your being generally disliked by your colleagues and subordinates because of your rough sarcastic & overbearing manner – It seems your Private Secretaries have agreed to behave like school boys & 'take what's coming to them' & then escape out of your presence shrugging their shoulders – Higher up, if an idea is suggested (say at a conference) you are supposed to be so contemptuous that presently no ideas, good or bad, will be forthcoming.

The decisive leaders who are most likely to avoid succumbing to acquired hubris syndrome have people in their lives, like Clementine Churchill or just people they respect whose mere presence reminds them not to get above themselves. They are also usually those who are careful to retain a personal modesty as they stay in power, to keep their previous lifestyle and to eschew the trappings of power. They try to consult carefully even if during that process they may not alter their opinions. Above all, in a democracy, they accept that the inbuilt institutional checks and balances should be scrupulously respected and make little or no attempt to circumvent them, whether in Cabinet or Parliament.

Disillusionment with politicians has grown markedly in recent years and some people seem to think all politicians are hubristic. But this is not the case. Chamberlain probably developed hubris syndrome in 1937-39. Most post-war heads of government in the USA and the UK, Truman, Attlee, Eisenhower, Macmillan, Douglas-Home, Ford, Carter, Callaghan, Reagan, Major and Bush Sr showed no signs of hubris. Kennedy's cynicism curbed any hubris and his mood was affected by the steroids and amphetamines he was being given by his doctors.[6a] Lyndon Johnson's hubris can be put down to a diagnosis of bipolar disorder.[6b] Any hubris in Eden was short lived and due to his illness, when he was being given a mixture of amphetamine and Benzedrine.[6c]

Heads of government likely to have developed hubris syndrome in the last century can be found among democrats as well as dictators. But I have not labelled anyone as having hubris syndrome who had a previous history of depression or possible personality disorder. For example, Theodore Roosevelt was hubristic and has been diagnosed as having had bipolar disorder,[7] but as with Churchill I have considerable doubt over the diagnosis. Woodrow Wilson and Richard Nixon were increasingly hubristic but Wilson suffered severe brain damage as a result of hypertension and Nixon has been diagnosed as an alcoholic. Many dictators were hubristic including Stalin, Hitler, Mao, Pol Pot, Amin and Mugabe, but none of these can be described as normal and some have questions as to whether they had or have personality disorders or mental illnesses.

Franklin Roosevelt looked as if he might be taken over by hubris syndrome when, in 1937, he fought and lost a battle with Congress over the Judicial Branch Reorganisation Plan, affecting the nomination of justices to the Supreme Court. But, fortunately, he had a sense of humour and a certain cynicism, which meant he never lost his moorings in the democratic system. Raymond Moley, who knew Roosevelt well from 1928 until 1936, analysed the problem of 'mental intoxication' that comes with power when exercised in isolation over long periods:

> Until the very end of my association with Roosevelt I hoped that his quality of pragmatism would keep some of the windows of his mind open. I finally found . . . that he himself was slamming shut windows. He developed a very special method of reassuring himself of his own pre-conceptions . . . Ultimately, of course, a man closed off by one means or another from free opinion and advice suffers a kind of mental intoxication. He lives in a world of ideas generated only by himself, a world of make-believe.[8]

Against that assessment, one has to recognise Roosevelt's personal determination, ruthlessness, guile and optimism, which enabled America – in the midst of the Great Depression – to overcome its troubles: he famously said at his first inauguration, 'The only thing we have to fear is fear itself.' Bold, brash, convincing, despite the recession continuing through the first four years, Roosevelt, in 1936, won 61% of the popular vote for his second term and went on to be the only four-term president. In the words of Jeff Shesol in his book *Supreme Power*[9] after the second inauguration, the United States "was now closer to one-party rule than it had been since Reconstruction". Then the president in early February 1937 announced publicly that he planned to pack the Supreme Court and was asking Congress, where the Senate contained 76 Democrats, to enlarge the court to 15. He had every intention of adding six liberals to the bench to stop in one fell swoop the court's majority obstructing his New Deal. Yet on 22 July 1937 the Senate rejected the Court Bill by 70 votes to 20. Roosevelt's defeat, so went the perceived wisdom, was easy to explain. "Why would Roosevelt embrace an idea as preposterous as packing the court? Hubris. What made him think he could get away with it? Hubris. Why did he refuse to listen to reason? Hubris. Why did he keep fighting when he had already lost (or won)? Hubris."[10]

It is amazing that over seventy years later we have this book challenging with great perception the perceived wisdom of the day arguing in great detail that hubris "alone is an insufficient answer to the question of what went wrong . . .", it was not a choice that Roosevelt made impulsively. It may have been driven – to a dangerous degree – by ego and emotion, but it was also the product of reason. It may have been wrong, but it was not rash. Neither was it made in a vacuum.

I do not believe President Franklin Roosevelt developed

hubris syndrome. He cheerily said to the cabinet immediately after the Senate defeat that he intended to have a great deal of fun in the months ahead and it was time for the country to laugh again. In August he cocked a snook at the Senate by nominating for a vacancy amongst the nine members of the Supreme Court one of their own, Senator Black, knowing they would feel unable to reject him at their hearings even though he had been an ardent supporter of packing the court. In acting in this way, Roosevelt showed the value of a cynical sense of humour acting as a check on his hubris. It is almost like being able to open a tap to relieve a mounting pressure to develop the condition.

Yet why did Roosevelt essentially make a major misjudgement of the Senate's reaction over packing the court? The answer, in as much as there can be any one explanation, probably lies in the death in April 1936 of Louis Howe. Ever since Roosevelt was a state senator in Albany, Howe had been his indispensable adviser. He had a room of his own in Roosevelt's homes in Manhattan and Hyde Park; also in the executive mansion in Albany and then the White House. No-one else spoke as frankly to Roosevelt as Howe. "You damned fool", "Goddammit, Franklin, you can't do that", or "*Mein Gott*! That's the stupidest idea I ever heard of" are but a sample of what he said.[11] Shesol describes Howe as "Roosevelt's balance wheel". He could challenge the president on many fronts or as Howe put it, "My job is to supply the toe-holds".

In assessing politicians for hubris syndrome I found a number of "toe holders", apart from Clementine Churchill with her husband. Andrew Bonar Law's absence, on health grounds, from Lloyd George's Coalition Cabinet from March 1921, was a great loss to Lloyd George and an important factor in him developing hubris syndrome. He adopted a growing belief that he was indispensable until he was disowned by his Conservative coalition partners in 1922.[12] William Whitelaw also provided a check on Margaret Thatcher. She only really developed hubris syndrome when he left the Cabinet two years before she was ousted by her own MPs in 1990.

Margaret Thatcher's career is almost a model case of a political leader succumbing to hubris syndrome, although she never displayed all of the symptoms. In 1979 when she became Prime Minister, she was not very hubristic though there were a few signs that she might have been susceptible in the way she divided her colleagues into 'them and us' and was dismissive of consensus. For the first two years she was careful to keep a large number of dissenting voices in the Cabinet and when confronted by the miners in an industrial dispute she was likely to lose, in 1981, she beat a retreat, albeit temporarily, until confronting them in 1984. The decisive event which was to change the nature of her premiership was the invasion of the Falkland Islands by Argentina in 1982. Although few British Prime Ministers would have done as she did and sent a naval task force down to the southern Atlantic to retrieve a small archipelago of little strategic significance, the decision itself was not hubristic. I know from my own conversations with her during the Falklands War that, while utterly determined, she was surprisingly cautious and in private she was more anxious than belligerent. Her 'rejoice, rejoice' statement on the steps of Number 10, following the landing of British troops on South Georgia, is often quoted as an example of hubris, but it was as much relief as exaltation.

Thatcher's success over the Falklands, though, and her inevitable victory in the subsequent general election, undoubtedly boosted her self-confidence. She began to dispense with colleagues who disagreed with her and to surround herself with those who shared her views. During the year-long miners' strike, which started in March 1984, she was not yet hubristic, but determined. She planned for it with great care, building up coal stocks before taking on the miners' leader, Arthur Scargill. Indeed she never lost her commitment to the importance of detail.

But the very fact that she had succeeded over the Falklands and the miners in the face of conventional wisdom, which would have had her compromise on both, meant that she became dangerously confident about her own judgement and contemp - tuous of other people's, especially after her third election victory in 1987. Her insistence on introducing the poll tax perfectly illustrates how she was succumbing to hubris syndrome. The tax was almost universally regarded as unfair but she was convinced it was not and ploughed on with the policy. Even a leader as self-confident as Churchill recoiled from such hubris. In preparing the Conservative manifesto for the 1950 election he cursorily dismissed the complaint of a young member of the party's

Research Department, Reginald Maudling, that a particular proposal was unfair; but when Maudling had the temerity to come back with the observation that the 'British people' would regard it as unfair, Churchill paused and remarked, 'Ah! That is a horse of a very different colour!' The proposal was dropped. But the weight of mere public opinion after her 1987 electoral victory was not something that would stop Thatcher in her tracks. Even here, though, she did not demonstrate that cavalier inattention to detail which is often symptomatic of the syndrome. Her Chancellor, Nigel Lawson, who opposed the poll tax, makes clear in his memoirs that there were extensive studies conducted about the pros and cons of the tax before it was introduced and that colleagues were very fully consulted. But the momentum behind it was undoubtedly Thatcher's unwavering conviction that it was 'right'. On a more comical level it started to become clear that she was suffering the effects of hubris when she greeted the arrival of her first grandchild with the remark: 'We have become a grandmother!'

By 1989 her grasp of the realities in which she was operating seemed to be deserting her. When the Berlin Wall came down in November, she refused to recognise that the reunification of East and West Germany would come immediately on to the political agenda. An underlying fear of a larger Germany developed into her privately talking emotionally about a Fourth Reich. She warned President George H. W. Bush that 'if we are not careful, the Germans will get in peace what Hitler couldn't get in the war',[13] a quite extraordinary remark. The fact that she totally miscalculated the speed of the political imperative that was driving German reunification was one of the signs that her political judgement was being jeopardised by her political prejudices and that her self-confidence was overriding her caution.

Full-blown hubris became evident on 30 October 1990, when she returned to the House of Commons from Rome after a meeting of the European Union's heads of government, where she had issued a series of statements in a press conference on what she would not agree to accept. The scene in the Commons was well described later by the *Guardian*'s political commentator, Hugo Young:

'Returning home, she had not cooled off. True, as quite often happened in the Thatcher decade, the relevant Whitehall officials effected a certain 'hosing down', so that the text of what she read out was controlled. But in answer to questions, it became in its monosyllabic brutality, the rubric of one of her most famous parliamentary moments, leaping with rage, ringing round the chamber, startling even those who in eleven years had much experience of the Thatcher vocabulary on Europe. 'No! No! No!' she bawled, her eyes seemingly directed to the fields and seas, the hills and the landing-grounds, where the island people would never surrender.' [14]

Thatcher's over-the-top performance that day in Parliament did not go down well with her Conservative MPs. I described her in my autobiography as being 'on an emotional high and the adrenalin was pumping round her system as she handbagged every federalist proposal'.[15] In their absolute certainty of view and the uncompromising manner in which they were expressed, her Eurosceptic words brought to mind the famous crude headline in the *Sun* newspaper about the then President of the European Commission, 'Up Yours Delors'.

One figure particularly upset by her performance was her deputy, Sir Geoffrey Howe, an enthusiastic European. He had been her loyal first Chancellor of the Exchequer and architect of the Thatcherite economic policies of her government. He had then been Foreign Secretary only to be moved again to be Leader of the House. But Thatcher had become increasingly contemptuous of his mild manner and her willingness to scorn and humiliate him publicly in Cabinet embarrassed even her thickest-skinned colleagues. This was hubris in its rawest form and Howe was ready to act as nemesis. His resignation speech in the House of Commons was all the more devastating because of the modest manner of its delivery, and within a month Thatcher had been forced out of office.

The political tragedy for Margaret Thatcher came about because she had pitted herself against her own source of power in Parliament, the Conservative MPs. She had reached a stage where she was not only not listening to her parliamentary colleagues but had become contemptuous of their views. Majority opinion in the parliamentary party was frequently flouted or manipulated. People of substance, who well knew that Cabinet government was a great constitutional safeguard, had allowed this situation to develop over the years, to the detriment of the British democratic system. The Cabinet had been reduced in stature and in quality. It was not just because she was a woman that the Cabinet had been so supine but it was a material factor. With the Cabinet too weak to act, it was left to the Conservative MPs to show their power. A leader who had won three general elections was removed – not by the nation's voters but within the rules of a parliamentary democracy by her party's own MPs. For those who believe in representative democracy and decisive leadership it was a perfect example of the democratic control mechanisms over a leader's hubris actually working. Thatcher and her friends preferred to categorise it as treachery and referred to it as a political assassination. But nemesis is the almost inevitable consequence of a democratic leader succumbing to hubris syndrome.

Bush, Blair and the war in Iraq

An example, in different forms, of hubris syndrome in operation is provided in the manner and conduct of the US President, George W. Bush, and the British Prime Minister, Tony Blair, when deciding to go to war in Iraq and in handling its aftermath. The evidence for my interpretation is derived not only from the mass of knowledge, made public about how these events came about but also, in the case of Blair, from my own personal dealings with him on Iraq between 1998 and 2002. Others later, with the perspective of a greater distance from this period of history, will be better placed to draw definitive conclusions. But contemporary interpretations of history can sometimes help those making historical assessments when they feel the imme - diacy of events and have personal knowledge of the participants. The disadvantage is that one is personally involved. We all have prejudices. It is helpful, therefore, to provide in summary form why in 2003, I supported regime change in Iraq.

In the summer of 1978, without any prior warning, a former Prime Minister of Iraq was assassinated on the streets of London. I was then Foreign Secretary and it was through this event that I first became aware of the nature of Saddam Hussein. He was the most powerful man in Baghdad, though not yet president of Iraq. In a very short space of time it became clear to the police and the British intelligence and secret services, MI5 and MI6, that Saddam was personally deeply implicated in the killing.

There have been many articles attempting to analyse Saddam Hussein. One profile stated that it was 'this political personality constellation – messianic ambition for unlimited power, absence of conscience, unconstrained aggression, and a paranoid outlook – that makes Saddam so dangerous. Conceptualised as malignant narcissism.'[1] A Swiss physician, Dr Pierre Rentchnick,[2] who was struck by the slowness of Saddam's responses on television in November 1990, talked to two British physicians who were passing through Geneva. They claimed that he was being treated with lithium for bipolar disorder and that he had suffered two depressive episodes, one during Iraq's eight-year war with Iran and the other in the autumn of 1990.[3] Yet at no time during his trial in Iraq did Saddam use mental illness as a mitigating factor in his defence, nor did the Iraqi Special Tribunal show any interest in exploring any mental illness before sentencing him to death by hanging in 2006.

In 1980 the world, and in particular Presidents Carter and Reagan and Prime Minister Thatcher, were wrong to raise so little objection to Saddam's totally unjustified invasion of Iran. Reagan and Thatcher were right, in 1981, however, to condemn Israel albeit very mildly for pre-emptively attacking the Osirak nuclear reactor in Iraq. Israel would be wrong in 2012 to attack Iran unilaterally, that requires Security Council authority.

Every UN member state has the right to take up arms in self defence; but that denotes a declaration of war. It cannot be right, let alone legal, to launch a pre-emptive attack without at least going first to the Security Council saying that existing sanctions are not halting the programme of nuclear weapons production and seeking a resolution declaring the situation to be a threat to the peace, without which the State of Israel should not act unilaterally.

During the Iran–Iraq War (1980–88) it became ever clearer that Saddam was using gas against Iranian troops. He also used it against Kurdish citizens in 1988 in Halabja, where for two days Iraqi jets dropped a hydrogen cyanide compound, developed with the help of a German company. More than 5,000 civilians were killed. Shamefully, the CIA sent out a briefing note to its embassies stating that the gas might have been dropped by the Iranians.[4] With this genocide against his fellow countrymen, Saddam's conduct passed a threshold which challenged the very purposes of the United Nations. The lack of tough, retaliatory, sanctions against him by the Security Council coupled with the world's low-key protests were indefensible, immoral and in clear breach of the 1948 UN Convention on Genocide.

British and American acquiescence in the Iraqi invasion of Iran owed everything to the practice of a form of realpolitik, explicable only in terms of hoping that by helping to keep the war going for eight years the Iranian revolution would burn itself out. But the zealotry of Iran's leaders continued unabated. It would have been in the wider interests of the USA and the UK to uphold the rule of international law in 1980 and penalise Saddam. We paid the price for not doing so when Iraq invaded Kuwait in 1990, whereupon we felt obliged to mount a major military intervention. When Iraqi troops went south to the Kuwait–Saudi border, within 200 miles of the Saudi city Dhahran, President Bush Sr was absolutely right to respond by offering to position American troops in Saudi Arabia.

The Iraqi army was forced out of Kuwait in February 1991. In the spring of that year, following UN Resolution 688, the USA, France and the UK imposed two no-fly zones, one over northern Iraq to protect the Kurds and over southern Iraq, to protect the Marsh Arabs. It was that action that created the precedent for the no-fly zone over Libya in 2011 that led to the ousting of the Gaddafi regime.

It is easy to forget that on 24 September 1991 UN inspectors in Baghdad found a large number of documents detailing Iraq's nuclear weapons programme in a building opposite a major hotel used by foreign journalists. On 6 July 1992 a UN humanitarian aid convoy in northern Iraq was attacked by Saddam's forces. Travelling in that convoy was Danielle Mitterrand, a prominent humanitarian activist and wife of the French President. Saddam also refused UN inspectors access to a building, an act which the Security Council declared 'a material and unacceptable breach of the provisions of Resolution 687'. Then a week later the Iraqis declined to participate in the UN Boundary Commission, charged with demarcating the Kuwait–Iraq border. The US administration believed that the escalation of events in Iraq was deliberately timed to coincide with the Balkan crisis and the lead-up to the US presidential election. In August the USA, the UK and France consulted in Washington on taking action against Iraq. President Bush began to be attacked in the campaign for not having ended Saddam Hussein's regime the year before, many Democrats conveniently forgetting how many of their senators had voted against taking military action. On 19 October 1992 Iraq featured in the final presidential debate. It was raised by the third candidate, Ross Perot, and gave Bill Clinton the opportunity to talk about 'cuddling Saddam Hussein when there was no reason to do it'.

The US air forces, which King Fahd of Saudi Arabia had controversially allowed to be deployed in his country as part of the campaign to oust Saddam from Kuwait in 1990, remained there afterwards, to enforce the no-fly zones and to constrain Saddam's border provocations. Before King Fahd's decision to accept US forces was announced, Osama bin Laden, himself a Saudi, tried to see the King to oppose the decision but was seen instead by Prince Sultan, the Saudi defence minister. Bin Laden hated Saddam, whom he considered a non-believer though both were Sunni Muslims. Bin Laden had been in Afghanistan through most of the 1980s fighting against the Soviet Union and had become a celebrity in Saudi Arabia. He offered to recruit an army of mujahideen to defend Saudi Arabia and claimed millions of Muslims would rally to the cause. Prince Sultan listened for nearly an hour before politely rejecting bin Laden's offer. When the news reached bin Laden that the Americans were coming into Saudi Arabia he denounced the King. In March 1991 he called for the overthrow of the monarchy and in April, fearing arrest, he left Saudi Arabia for the Pakistan border with Afghanistan.

Saddam steadily began to increase his malign political influence in the region despite, or perhaps for some countries because of, the US and UK military actions. He ruthlessly campaigned against any UN sanctions by refusing to let urgent medical supplies reach Iraqi children, while blaming the UN for their absence. Through the 1990s the World Health Organization reported a steep rise in prenatal mortality rates and avoidable illnesses among Iraqi children. In part, as a result, it became increasingly hard to carry support in international forums for the implementation of sanctions. The UN Security Council tolerated Jordan and Turkey's evasion of oil sanctions, rather than giving them financial compensation. This meant that the USA and the UK were undermining their own positions. Increasingly, over the years, in a climate of hypocrisy, international political opposition to sanctions against Iraq grew. France opportunistically withdrew its military aircraft from policing the no-fly zones and, with Russia and Germany, began to ignore UN economic sanctions, instead building up commercial relations with Iraq.

The USA and the UK were able to contain Iraqi aircraft, tanks and helicopters from crossing the line in the north, but in the south the Marsh Arabs were driven out by Saddam and their habitat flooded. The world appeared to want to forget that the

US-led multilateral force in 1991 had deliberately chosen not to capture Baghdad and had, for humanitarian reasons, stopped firing on retreating Iraqi forces, relying instead on the ceasefire terms endorsed by the UN Security Council. It is to the shame of the UN structures, and particularly the Security Council, that these ceasefire resolutions were consistently flouted and that the deteriorating health statistics for children in Iraq were not properly explained. The Security Council knew that health priorities were manipulated inside Iraq by Saddam for purely political purposes.

On 26 June 1993 Saddam brushed off an attack on his military intelligence headquarters by Tomahawk missiles. This attack was ordered by President Clinton in retaliation for the discovery of an Iraqi secret intelligence service assassination attempt on the former President George Bush and his family when he was visiting Kuwait on 15–18 April. Two women who really mattered to the man who would be president, George W. Bush, were in Kuwait, his mother Barbara and wife Laura. It is not hard to believe that the iron entered his soul then in relation to Saddam and he identified him as an evil person, which he was. Clinton's action relied on the UN resolutions dating from 1990 and 1991 which declared Iraq to be a threat to world peace. Much of the legal arguments about attacking Iraq in 2003 stem from those UN declarations that Iraq continued to be a threat to world peace. Saddam's deployment of some 80,000 troops near Kuwait in October 1994 merely confirmed this view.

Saddam was exploiting the perceived weakness of the United States particularly, after Clinton had removed US forces from Somalia, following the shooting down of two Black Hawk helicopters. Al-Qaeda was also building up its strength in Somalia. A failed plot by generals inside Iraq to kill Saddam in June 1996 further emboldened him, and in August he plotted with one Kurdish faction to attack another at Arbis inside the northern no-fly zone. But by this time the Clinton administration could not get permission from either the Turks or the Saudis to use their airbases to attack Iraq. Instead, on 3 September, the USA launched forty Tomahawk cruise missiles to destroy an Iraqi air defence installation in the southern no-fly zone. But this was 500 miles from Arbis: the inadequacy of this massive response showed how little Saddam was being contained by those who had defeated him in 1991. He might not have been capable of attacking his neighbours but his crimes against humanity did not lessen. And he felt confident enough to defy the UN by refusing to cooperate with its inspectors monitoring his com - mitment after 1991 not to develop weapons of mass destruction (WMD). In 1998, the UN inspectors were withdrawn as a result of his non-cooperation. US and UK aircraft were continuously shot at during the next twelve years until the invasion in 2003. If this was containment it was a strange and new use of the word that had been applied by George Kennan to Russia when anticipating the Cold War.

Despite what Saddam did to the Shi'ites and Kurds in Iraq over these years, there was no readiness in the USA or elsewhere to use military power to topple him. The UN Security Council failed to alleviate the rise in infant mortality and the deteriorating health and social condition of millions of Iraqis. The corruption surrounding the UN's oil-for-food programme was revealed in a report commissioned by the then secretary general, Kofi Annan, and chaired by Paul Volcker, the former head of the US Federal Reserve. It was published on 14 September 2005. It showed that Annan was aware of a kickback scheme involving 2,500 companies in the oil-for-food programme 'at least as early as February 2001'. He was criticised in the report for never subsequently mentioning the kickbacks to the Iraqi government in his quarterly reports to the UN. In behind all the kickbacks, French companies sold Saddam humanitarian 'assistance' to the value of $3 billion, while Russian companies made deals with Iraq to the value of $19 billion in an overall oil-for-food programme worth in excess of $100 billion. That the Security Council countries knew about the kickbacks is not an excuse for the secretary general and the UN Secretariat remaining silent. The standing of the UN was gravely damaged by the complicity of the Secretariat, who should have forced the issue out into the open and made the Security Council face up to the duplicity and criminality involved.

All these actions by Saddam Hussein made it clear to me, that not only was containment not working, but that the USA and the UK's policy was not just failing but was doing much collateral harm inside Iraq as Saddam deliberately ensured that

UN sanctions were used against his people, particularly sick children. Sanctions were being undermined also by Russia, France and Germany, and there was no readiness on the Security Council to uphold the previous UN resolutions. Military action to remove Saddam was, I felt, the only alternative, assassination attempts having failed. But this meant deploying forces sufficient not just to topple Saddam but also to conduct a nation-building operation in the aftermath.

After 9/11 the USA developed, once again, the political will to return to the region with substantial ground forces. Any existing Iraqi WMD should, I felt, be dealt with in the aftermath of toppling Saddam. The existence of WMD was not, in my view, nor should it have been allowed to become, the sole reason for justifying an invasion. Ensuring WMD could never return was part and parcel of regime change for Saddam Hussein was inextricably part of the problem, which I explained to Jack Straw on the telephone as the reasons why on 18 March 2003, I was in favour of using military force to topple Saddam Hussein. The tragedy was that the handling of the aftermath of a successful invasion was so disastrous. Tony Blair's continued failure to recognize this publicly has been a Greek tragedy haunting him as he desperately tries to maintain his political stature in 2012.

Even his reasonable policy to persuade Gaddafi in 2004 to forego WMD and terrorism has come unstuck in his hands because of his close personal identification with Gaddafi's regime. As Prime Minister visiting and then flamboyantly hugging Gaddafi was unnecessary and personally humiliating, particularly so in the light of the successful UN-supported no-fly zone and NATO in 2011 which ousted Gaddafi's regime.

On 18 September 2011 the *Sunday Telegraph* published extracts from documents found in Libya which revealed that Blair, after he had resigned as Prime Minister, held meetings with Gaddafi which had not previously been reported. Among the documents was a letter on official notepaper from the 'Office of the Quartet Representative', the job Tony Blair had taken in the established role of helping with the economic development of Palestine. The letter stated "Mr Blair is delighted that the Leader is likely to be able to see him during the afternoon of 10 June" [2008]. This was followed by another meeting in April 2009 and then in August of that year, the 'Lockerbie Bomber', Abdelbaset al-Megrahi was released from prison in Scotland. Another meeting between Blair and Gaddafi it is claimed took place in June 2010.

Questions were asked about the propriety of the visits. A former British Ambassador to Libya claimed that Blair was 'clearly using his Downing Street contacts to further his business interests'. That the Libyans apparently flew him in and out of their country together with a trustee of Blair's US Faith Foundation, who was also present at the meetings with Gaddafi, added weight to the ambassador's assertion. But in fairness Blair was I am sure, trying to attract Libyan funds for investment in Palestine in addition to his other activities.

The worrying feature was that Blair's hubris prevented him from seeing that Gaddafi was worse than disreputable and definitely not someone he should be personally involved with at such an intimate level. Equally concerning was that Blair's role in the Quartet meant he was circumscribed to representing the UN, the US, Russia and the European Union in the Middle East not his own personal and financial interests.

Personal contacts with Tony Blair 1998–2001, prior to the Iraq War

Although the war in Iraq was overwhelmingly an American-led enterprise it makes sense to begin by discussing the evolution of Tony Blair's approach to the problem, since he came to power in May 1997, three and half years before George W. Bush entered the White House.

My first significant meeting with Tony Blair was on 15 July 1996. It was a private meeting at his home, when he was leader of the opposition. It was a long meeting during which it became clear he was trying to persuade me to endorse, effectively to rejoin, the Labour Party. I was enthusiastic about his creation of 'New Labour' and the fact that he had adopted many of the policies of the Social Democratic Party, of which I was a founder member and leader from 1983-87 and 1988-90. Now unlike when fighting his by-election he supported membership of the European Union and the UK's nuclear deterrent. One important area on which in our conversation it became clear that we differed strongly was the degree of European federal integration. He favoured far greater institutional integration which I was against. More fundamentally I believed it was far too early for the UK even to contemplate adopting the euro. Yet Blair was both enthusiastic for entry and ignorant of the potentially adverse consequences.

Despite the generosity of the offer and the chance of ending the divisions with the social democratic family in the UK, I decided to stay an independent social democrat crossbench member of the House of Lords in order to remain free to oppose, on an all-party basis, euro entry. In retrospect I regard it as one of the wisest decisions I have made not to be drawn into the Blair orbit.

All three main party leaders in 1997 were forced by public opinion to pledge a referendum before euro entry. Prime Minister John Major, readily; in the case of Tony Blair and Charles Kennedy, with extreme reluctance. It soon became clear after the General Election and after just winning a referendum on Welsh devolution that a cautious Tony Blair was not going to embark on a referendum on the euro in his first term. The danger point of a euro referendum was greatest in 2003 on the back of what was referred to in Downing Street in 2002, as a "Baghdad bounce". The plan was in the wake of a great victory over Saddam Hussein for Tony Blair, with high opinion poll ratings, to confront Gordon Brown and make his continuance as either Chancellor of the Exchequer or Foreign Secretary on his support for a "yes to euro entry" campaign. It was recognised in the Treasury that much of Gordon Brown's hesitation over euro entry was linked to his rivalry with Blair. Brown was never like

Nigel Lawson when Chancellor, in principle against the very concept of a single European currency. The stalwart opposition to euro entry at that time in the Treasury was Brown's key political adviser Ed Balls, the architect of the so-called "five tests" and now as an MP, Labour's 'shadow' Chancellor.

I discussed Iraq with Blair on 2 March 1998 in Downing Street and, as a sign of my depth of feeling about the country, gave him a book about the Kurds written by Jonathan Randal, an experienced war correspondent with the *Washington Post*. It reflected my deep concern at the time and why I believed the Kurdish position, so long ignored by the Western democracies, had become so crucial. I hoped Blair would read this brilliant book, as it posed many questions for the future. For example, in discussing how the aftermath of the defeat of the Iraqi forces in 1991 had left much to be desired, Randal anticipated all and more of what was to come in 2003:

> The American planning was a hodgepodge of naivety and *realpolitik*, more tactics than strategy, seemingly consistent only if its peculiar assumptions were correct . . . No-one should have been surprised by anything that happened from 2 August 1990 when Iraq invaded and occupied Kuwait to the end of the following March, when Saddam Hussein crushed the Shia and Kurdish uprisings.[5]

I followed up the concerns I had expressed at that meeting with a letter to Blair on 12 November, arguing that there had to be a political strategy involving the Kurds to help topple Saddam Hussein. Blair replied, 'We are not working to bring down Saddam Hussein and his regime. It is not for us to say who should be President of Iraq, however much we might prefer to see a different government in Baghdad.' This exchange encapsulated the UK's particular problem: successive British governments have felt legally bound to use wording on regime change based on a particularly inflexible interpretation of the UN Charter. That position I believe the UK must re-examine. Easier to do now after the successful constrained intervention in Libya in 2011. Libya was a humanitarian intervention, but one which could only achieve its objectives after regime change. It planned to tilt the balance of fighting between Libyans on the ground with no occupying armies, as requested by the Arab League and authorised by the Security Council.

Following the withdrawal of UN inspectors from Iraq in 1998 in response to Saddam's non-cooperation, the USA and Britain launched a four-day bombing campaign against Iraqi targets. The military operation was undertaken, as in 1993 and 1996, and again in 2002 and 2003, with the USA and the UK claiming the authority of the UN resolutions passed in 1990 and 1991 and in addition UNSCR 1205, passed in 1998. No country on the Security Council formally challenged the authority of the US and UK action by putting the matter to the vote, which they could have done.

Blair asked me and my wife to dinner at 10 Downing Street on 18 December 1998, which happened to coincide with the third evening of the bombing blitz. The main reason for the invitation was Blair's wish to dissuade me from establishing an organisation later called New Europe, which from 1999-2005, opposed the UK joining the euro, and having succeeded was then wound up. But we also discussed Iraq at some length. His mood was quite different from what it seems to have been two days earlier when, over dinner with Cherie and two close friends, Barry Cox and his wife, he was reported to be 'distinctly nervous'.[6]

At dinner with Cherie on the 18th I found him relaxed, almost laid back. He had started well as Prime Minister, particularly in handling Northern Ireland, and this proved to be his substantive success. There was no undue hyperactivity. He did not excuse himself to get an update on the attacks that had been launched and I found him cool, rational, and anything but hubristic. He was ready to discuss the complexity of the relations between the Shi'ite majority and the Kurds and Sunnis in Iraq in some detail but he was still not very knowledgeable about them and he had obviously not read Randal's book which I had given him. We agreed that the situation which allowed Saddam to stay in power was totally unsatisfactory and shared the frustration about UN limitations within which he, Blair, felt formally he had to operate. The USA's Congressional resolution for regime change, called the Iraq Liberation Act, had meanwhile been passed by an overwhelming majority, which President Clinton did not veto. The challenge seen by us both was Saddam's continuation in power, not WMD, which were only briefly mentioned though we both believed they were still present in Iraq. The US and the UK dropped more than 600 bombs and launched 415 cruise missiles against Iraqi targets during the four days, killing an estimated 1,400 members of Iraq's Republican Guard. The action, which had been targeted on some nuclear facilities, was later assessed as having set back Saddam's nuclear weapons programme by two years.[7] France and Russian could have challenged the action on legal grounds in the Security Council then as they did later in 2002-3.

Clinton, though committed to the Congressional resolution calling for regime change in Iraq, was never likely to authorise the full military invasion necessary to achieve this. American public opinion was not ready for military re-engagement on the ground in Iraq. The failed impeachment of Clinton over Monica Lewinsky in February 1999 had weakened his authority to go to the American people and demand action and this may have been a factor also when deciding what to do with the growing threat to the USA of Osama bin Laden and al-Qaeda. The priority issue for military action for NATO, in the year ahead, was Kosovo.

My next conversation with Blair was during the Kosovo crisis when NATO was engaging in air attacks on Serbia. On 16 April 1999, the Prime Minister unexpectedly rang me wanting a long and detailed talk about his anxieties over the deteriorating situation. The Serb military were still largely unaffected by the NATO bombing and he wanted to discuss my publicly stated views that we should from the outset have been prepared to use

NATO ground forces. Somewhat unconventionally, I was attacked by name for these views, along with Henry Kissinger, in an article by General Charles Guthrie, then the UK Chief of the Defence Staff.[8] This was a small but significant sign of the politicisation of the military that had started under Blair. Clinton's advisers had told him that Slobodan Milošević would fold if threatened and, when he did not, that bombing would do the trick in forty-eight, then seventy-two hours.[9] Eventually it took seventy-eight days of bombing and Boris Yeltsin's political intervention forcing Milošević to withdraw the Serbian armed forces and police negating the need for 'boots on the ground'.

I mentioned to Blair at an early stage that I was speaking from Berlin on an open line. He laughed and said he wanted anyone listening to know about his anxieties. Blair was surprisingly frank and we had an animated discussion. I sensed, however, for the first time a note of exaltation in his voice. Soon afterwards real tension developed between Blair and Clinton about the need to prepare to send in ground forces and on 21 April, Blair told Parliament that ground troops were an option.

On 24 April Blair made a speech in Chicago, in which he tried to identify the circumstances in which Britain 'should get actively involved in other people's conflicts' in defence of our values. Whatever its rights and wrongs, and in large part I agreed with it, what was irresponsible for such an important speech was how little examination of its implications took place in Whitehall. It was drafted by a professor of war studies, Lawrence Freedman, who was later appointed a member of the Iraq

Inquiry. Freedman was himself surprised that Blair made very few changes to his proposed text which is on the Iraq Inquiry website. Odd behaviour for an important speech.

One damaging side effect of Kosovo, in retrospect, was the mood of self-confidence and personal dominance that began to appear in Blair's handling of foreign affairs. Kosovo was Blair's first test in a big international crisis and unmistakable signs of hubristic attitudes were beginning to emerge. Clinton's aides mocked Blair's 'Churchillian tone'.[10] One official who saw him frequently said, 'Tony is doing too much, he's overdoing it and he's overplaying his hand.' At one stage, the President angrily told Blair to 'pull himself together' and halt 'domestic grandstanding'. He was starting to display excessive pride in his own judgements. A Clinton aide suggested Blair 'was sprinkling too much adrenalin on his cornflakes'.[11]

It is worth noting how often this hormone, adrenaline, called epinephrine in the USA and secreted by the medulla of the adrenal gland, is referred to when people discuss manic behaviour or hubris. But if there is any linkage it is a complex one embraced within the two-factor theory of emotion, where the adrenaline may produce a physiological arousal but there also needs to be a cognition to interpret the meaning of this arousal.[12]

After my telephone conversation with Blair from Berlin, I began to realise how personalised and very different his style of leadership was from the measured and structured style I had watched James Callaghan use as Prime Minister. Blair liked to claim he was following Margaret Thatcher's style of leadership, but this claim was false in many respects in particular her now well chronicled handling of the Falklands War. Unlike him, she had a formidable commitment to a political philosophy and she was renowned for her close attention to detail. But most of all, she was already experienced when she became Prime Minister, having served as a junior minister under Harold Macmillan and in Cabinet as Secretary of State for Education under Edward Heath. On taking office Blair was the most inexperienced British Prime Minister since Ramsay MacDonald in 1924, never having held any ministerial office before entering Number 10 and it showed. The same applies to David Cameron.

Furthermore, Blair had had no formal training or experience in management. He tried to make up for this by talking to management thinkers and seemed, according to an article in *Management Today*, to want to act like a chief executive: 'Fast on his feet, flexible in his thinking and able to make quick decisions, often taken on the hoof, in shirtsleeves, on the sofa, coffee latte in one hand, mobile phone in the other, running Great Britain PLC as if it were a City investment company.'[13] But the role of Prime Minister is not that of a chief executive and the UK government is not a company making profits for shareholders. Blair's chief of staff, Jonathan Powell, writes beguilingly but unconvincingly that the role should be more akin to that of Machiavelli, an Italian Prince who Powell believes is as misunderstood as is his own master, Tony Blair. "It is perhaps four hundred years too late to rehabilitate Machiavelli and perhaps twenty years too soon to persuade people to re-evaluate Tony Blair.[14] But neither Blair nor Powell had ever held responsibility for a government department and it is seen in both the naivety and inconsistencies of their analysis, and in how they ran Number 10.

The last chapter in Powell's book, *The New Machiavelli* is entitled 'The Arrogance of One Who Rises to Power in a Republic', a quote from Machiavelli. It is subtitled, 'Hubris and Leaving Office'. It discusses the merits of term limits fixed for eight years in the US Constitution or, as Powell believes, informal term limits of no more than ten years for the UK. Powell, however, goes on to write vacuously about "People's attention span is shorter now than in the past, the media are in the market for a new narrative, everyone is bored, and for the same reason that the shelf life of celebrities has become shorter and shorter, so has that of politicians." There is a superficiality to many of the recorded dialogues in his book. Rarely is there anything other than the assumption that politics is purely a personal issue of power.

Quite apart from the chronicling of what Tony said to Gordon and what Gordon said to Tony, not the most edifying aspect of their period in office, the book raises the key question perhaps unconsciously; was Blair afraid to sack or discipline Brown? There is also no discussion of the possibility that the style of government with its constant obsession with "presentation" might be contributing to people's attention span becoming shorter. Everything focuses on news management;

there is little discussion of government as a public good, nor of the responsibility of power. No questioning of why some other Prime Ministers did not have the same restlessness about their personal image. No admission that Cabinet government has virtues, that delegation of authority has strengths. In disparaging solidarity and collective responsibility there is little recognition that these are core beliefs for social democrats.

Machiavelli in one popular translation of *The Prince* writes: "Therefore, a prudent prince must hold to a third mode, choosing wise men in his state; and only to these should he give freedom to speak the truth to him, and of those things only that he asks about and nothing else. But, he should ask them about everything and listen to their opinions; then he should decide by himself, in his own mode . . ." A more explicit warning of hubris comes from Sophocles' *Antigone*, in which Haemon speaks to his father, Creon, the regent king. "I beg you, do not be unchange-able; do not believe that you alone can be right. The man who thinks that, the man who maintains that only he has the power to reason correctly, the gift to speak, the soul . . . A man like that, when you know him, turns out empty."

Powell's writing has within it an implicit assumption that hubris is an inevitable part of leadership and Blair's pre-occupation with when he should step down is part of it. In June 2002, Blair told his close advisers that he might retire at the next election. By May 2003 he was again agonising about whether to run for a third term or not. The pressure for Blair to leave began to build up in earnest in 2004. Then in the summer he told them he was going to serve a third term but would not seek a fourth and coyly revealed he had bought a £3.6 million house in the Bayswater district of London while contemplating resignation earlier in the year.

Like Blair, Thatcher had sought to accrete more power into No. 10 but to do so, she worked within the existing Cabinet structures. Even though she made considerable use of a personal foreign affairs adviser, Charles Powell, then a serving diplomat, the Cabinet Secretary remained a powerful independent figure. By contrast, Blair chose a formalised destruction of the Cabinet system. He started by appointing a political chief of staff, Jonathan Powell, the brother of Charles. His role was not just political and he was uniquely given the powers of a civil servant. This arrangement progressively undermined the authority of the Cabinet Secretary. Later, in 2001, and in the flush of victory after winning a second general election, Blair, with no parliamentary scrutiny, changed the whole basis of Cabinet government as it related to foreign and defence matters. A system which had evolved during the First World War was swept aside without a single serious objective study. This was not modernisation but hubristic vandalism, for which, as Prime Minister, Blair alone bears responsibility.

The new structure was deliberately designed by Blair to ensure he could exercise over international policy much the same powers as an American president. The Cabinet Office method of handling foreign and security matters had, until then, been designed to service the Cabinet as a whole. From the summer of

2001 onwards, the key officials and their staff on foreign affairs, defence and the European Union were brought into the political hothouse atmosphere of 10 Downing Street in two new secretariats.[15] The No. 10 secretariats were intended to service the Prime Minister alone, politically and strategically. Blair was to do much the same to the Joint Intelligence Committee (JIC), in terms of its working arrangements if not in terms of its formal structure. This new structure in No. 10 was designed to cause the progressive downgrading of the Foreign Office and the Ministry of Defence and their respective secretaries of state. It was an attempt to create a 'White House' as in the US with 'presidential' power emanating from 10 Downing Street.

A few months after the two secretariats were in place the new structure provided the means to project Blair's very personalised response to the 9/11 bombings in New York and Washington. 'A warning sign was the astonishing mixture of hubris and hysteria that ran through his speech to the Labour Party Conference immediately after the atrocity.'[16] He promised the American people: 'We were with you at the first, we will stay with you to the last.' The empty quality of such rhetoric was later revealed when British servicemen were withdrawn from Basra and the Americans took their place. The consequence of Blair's exclusive reliance on these new secretariats was to be the lack of objectivity, probity and collectivity which became the hallmarks of his misjudgements and incompetence in handling the aftermath of the 2001 invasion of Afghanistan and the 2003 invasion of Iraq.

There have, of course, been incompetent Prime Ministers before but Blair's incompetence was to be of a very particular sort. It was triggered by three characteristic symptoms of hubris: excessive self-confidence, restlessness and inattention to detail. A self-confidence that exclusively reserves decision-making to itself, does not seek advice and fails to listen to or is contemptuous of the wisdom of others, particularly if it conflicts with the leader's own viewpoint, is hubristic. If this is combined with an energy that is restless for action and is ready to intervene on the basis of a loose sense of the broader picture rather than the detailed study of all the relevant information, then serious mis - takes are almost inevitable. Such was to be the case in Blair's handling of affairs after 9/11: the misjudgements were those of hubristic incompetence and inattention to detail,

An article in the *Sunday Times* on 28 August 2011 describes Blair returning to Downing Street from Brighton on 9/11 where waiting for him were John Scarlett from MI6, who had only been the Chairman of the JIC for eight days, and Stephen Lander, head of MI5. Blair asked, "Who's done this?" Lander replied "The most likely is Osama bin Laden's organisation." Lander felt Afghanistan's Taleban was the most likely link. Blair was apparently taken aback. "If it's coming from Afghanistan did I know about this?" The spies coughed a little. "Well", Lander answered, "if you'd read the JIC material fully you would have come across some of this stuff." A JIC report from 16 July had warned that al-Qaeda operating from bases in Afghanistan was in the "final stages" of preparing an attack on the West, with

UK interests "at risk, including from collateral damage in attacks on US targets."

How to use specialist expertise within Departments is always an issue for Prime Ministers but there is no escape from wider reading and questioning. Also ordering further studies from briefing notes and JIC reports. That was simply not done in 2001 in No. 10 over Afghanistan and this was confirmed in an interview with Jonathan Powell for a BBC2 documentary shown in September 2011.

"In the aftermath it occurred to me how little we knew about the Taleban at all. 9/11 had happened and we had not really had the Taleban on our radar screen at all. So I walked down Whitehall to Waterstone's at Trafalgar Square and bought a copy of all the books I could find on the Taleban and the only one that was of any use was by Ahmed Rashid which is a very good book on the Taleban and the fight with the warlords. And I sat at my desk and read this for the next 12 hours – read the whole book – and Alastair and Tony were getting very jealous and wanted to have my copy and had to wait. Alastair got to read it first and then Tony after that and then we were all experts on the Taleban". [17]

Fortunately the British government did have within it considerable expertise. In the garden of the British Embassy in Washington on the day after 9/11 the heads of MI6, MI5 and GCHQ gathered and discussed, in the words of Eliza Manningham-Buller in her Reith Lecture in 2011 "the near-certainty of a war in Afghanistan to destroy al-Qaeda bases there and drive out the terrorists and their sponsors, the Taleban. We all saw that war in Afghanistan as necessary. And in Afghanistan documents and rudimentary laboratories were discovered showing the terrorists' keen interest in fulfilling bin Laden's stricture to acquire and use nuclear material. What none of us anticipated was that this unity of purpose would be tested by the decision of the US, supported by the UK, and others, after the rout of the Taleban, to invade Iraq. Saddam Hussein was a ruthless dictator and the world is better off without him. But his regime had nothing to do with 9/11 and despite an extensive search for links, none but the most trivial was found."

Bush and Blair after 9/11

George W. Bush, like Tony Blair, became head of government without having previously served in any national government post. It is true that he had been governor of Texas, but Texas is unusual in that its governor exercises much less executive power than those in most other American states. When Bush became president he started by saying he would appoint good people, delegate authority and hold them accountable for results – following best practice at Harvard Business School, which he had attended. Such an approach to government is the opposite of hubristic. So too was his characterisation of the foreign policy he promised when running for office: he said he wanted America's stance in the world to be 'strong but humble'.

In private, on the seventeenth day of the Bush Presidency, 5

February 2001, the new Secretary of Defense gave a far more self confident and American first assessment. Donald Rumsfeld said to his senior colleagues, 'Imagine what the region would look like without Saddam and with a regime that's aligned with US interests. It would change everything in the region and beyond it. It would demonstrate what US policy is all about.'[18] On 16 February 2001 Bush agreed that US and UK bombers, as part of the ongoing policy inherited from President Clinton's eight years in office, should hit Iraqi radar and command centres and on 10 August the USA and the UK again bombed three Iraqi defence sites. Press comment was low key. A month before 9/11 the president's daily intelligence brief was headed 'Bin Laden Determined to Strike in US'.

Whether or not Bush really did intend to be 'humble abroad' and not 'engage in nation-building' as well as being a delegating, hands-off leader will remain one of the unknowns of history. What is clear is that after 11 September 2001, or 9/11, that would have been an impossible stance for any American president to adopt. Initially Bush was shocked, as his face showed when, in a school in Florida, he was first told the news of a second aeroplane hitting the World Trade Center in New York. The outrage the American people felt immediately after 9/11 meant that they were ready to abandon the long-standing philosophical guidelines set down by John Quincy Adams when he was Secretary of State in 1821, and which the Vietnam experience had seemed to justify. America 'goes not abroad in search of monsters to destroy. She is the well wisher to the freedom and independence of all. She is the champion and vindicator only of her own.' From the moment Bush seized the portable loud hailer amid the devastation and rubble on 15 September and said, 'The people who knocked these buildings down will hear all of us soon,' he came to refer to himself as the 'decider'. He saw himself as a 'wartime president' and he saw his main priority as mobilising America for military action. In doing so his adoption of the phrase 'war on terror' was imprecise, even misleading, but it was designed in the immediate circumstances, to rally his country to face the foe which al-Qaeda presented. It is important to understand Bush's own interpretation of why he used the term 'war'. In his memoirs published in 2010 he writes "I admired Lincoln's moral clarity and resolve. The clash between freedom and tyranny, he said, was 'an issue which can only be tried by war, and decided by victory'. The war on terror would be the same."[19] In another passage he describes his meeting with Congressional leaders on 12 September: "Senator Tom Daschle, the Democratic majority leader, issued one cautionary note. He said I should be careful about the word *war* because it had such powerful implications. I listened to his concerns, but I disagreed. If four coordinated attacks by a terrorist network that had pledged to kill as many Americans as possible was not an act of war, then what was it? A breach of diplomatic protocol?"[20]

Soon Bush's self-image became inflated, promising 'to smoke 'em out and get 'em running' and on 16 September vowing to 'rid the world of evil doers'. This was not just talk, it truly represented his approach. He saw the war as a military war, like the First and Second World Wars. He had not recognised that those wars were a thing of the past and that wars now were, in the British General Rupert Smith's words, 'war amongst the people'. [21]

The will to take up arms internationally returned to America after 11 September 2001. Quite rightly, President Bush seized the moment. He chose to take action militarily against Afghanistan and its Taleban government, who had been sheltering al-Qaeda, the agents of 9/11. Once the al-Qaeda attacks on New York and Washington had taken place, few, anywhere in the world, doubted that military action against Afghanistan was the correct initial response. It should be remembered too that 9/11 was not, as many people in the world think, a personal reaction to Bush's policies or actions. Still less was it a direct result of the Arab–Israeli dispute: the planning for 9/11 had started at a time when President Clinton was actively involved in seeking a settlement between the Palestinian leader, Yasser Arafat, and the Israeli Prime Minister, Ehud Barak.

It is easy to overlook the fact too that Samuel Huntington's thesis *The Clash of Civilizations and the Remaking of World Order* had been published in the USA as far back as 1996 and that there had been a vigorous debate about Islamic fundamentalism well before 9/11. Al-Qaeda had taunted the US for running away from a confrontation in Somalia in 1993, years before George W Bush featured in international politics. To his credit, in the heightened tension immediately after 9/11, Bush spoke warmly of the many peace-loving Muslims within the USA and tried to reassure them. Also he did not repeat the mistake that President Roosevelt made after Pearl Harbor when Japanese nationals living in the USA had been interned as 'enemy aliens'.

But even though the invasion of Afghanistan was justified, worrying signs of a developing hubris within Bush emerged from the start of the campaign. In the first place, the longer-term problems of controlling the country after the invasion had been achieved were grossly underestimated from the outset. Furthermore Bush, by focusing on war and military ways of dealing with the new aspects of worldwide terrorism, allowed the Taleban and al-Qaeda to gain in stature and strength. [22] Bush policies departed from many established techniques for dealing with unstable states and the terrorists they often harbour. The side effects of the new techniques for prisoners, such as those used in Guantanamo, and the practice of rendition have actually served to breed terrorism. Disregarding the possibility that the consequences of their approach would actually worsen the problem they were trying to deal with is a characteristic of the hubris syndrome.

Yet the issues Bush had to face cannot be just ignored, particularly since we can now see that they have not been resolved. We need a new Geneva Convention to deal with combatants who come from or operate in dysfunctional states. We need stronger interpretative statements from the Security Council on the UN Charter for dealing with terrorist attacks. In some circumstances the right of self-defence might include regime change, even pre-emption, and it might be reasonable not to define that as retaliation. There should be a specific code of conduct to deal with interrogation procedures for people involved in terrorism. None of these questions – and there are many more – are comfortable to answer. The onus was on Bush and Blair, even if they considered themselves at war, to convince, with the truth, that the protection of citizens worldwide needed specific changes to the existing framework. By and large they failed to conduct such an exercise.

In the UK in addition to the Iraq War Inquiry, an attempt was made for Sir Peter Gibson to examine claims of British complicity in the torture of terror suspects abroad. A court case is now likely over alleged MI6 involvement in the case of Abdel Hakim Belhadj who in 2004, was regarded as a member of a jihadist organization but is now, in 2012, a military leader in the post Gaddafi government in Tripoli. There are other cases emerging from Libya. The Gibson inquiry will either have to be more open than was planned, or be dropped. But dealing with the secret intelligence services (SIS) openly is almost impossible.

Rendition, returning people to their country of origin, knowing that they may be tortured, according to Sir Richard Dearlove, the former head of MI6, 'would have been illegal under British common law'. So deniability became the way around this, according to the then head of CIA covert operations in Europe, speaking to the *Guardian* on 25 May 2007. After 9/11 military perspectives dominated anti-terrorism activity. Bush and Blair both externally and internally never realised or had forgotten that terrorist actions are primarily taken to send a message. Terrorists seek revenge, renown and reaction, the 'three Rs', brilliantly analysed by an Irish Harvard professor who has long studied the subject. [23]

The case of Moazzam Begg, a British citizen of Pakistani descent, reported in detail on 15 June 2006 in the *New York Times*, illustrates many of the complexities which those who are trying to prevent more bombings such as 9/11, Madrid and London deal with on a day-to-day basis. They have to try to collect a myriad of small pieces of information that only when put together, like a jigsaw puzzle, produce the preventive intelligence they need. Begg was an immigrant educated in the UK in Birmingham. He went to Pakistan and Afghanistan in late 1993. Arrested in 1994, the charges were later dropped for lack of evidence. He became, however, a police suspect because they found a night-vision sight, a bulletproof vest and what a news report called extremist literature. He returned to Britain in 1998 and received a visit from MI5 in his bookshop, which was searched and raided again in February 2000. He was arrested under the Prevention of Terrorism Act but quickly released without charge. He moved with his family to Afghanistan in July 2001. Arrested in Pakistan on 31 January 2002, he was transferred to a prison camp in Kandahar in Afghanistan, to Bagram airbase, then to Guantanamo. Designated in 2003 as eligible for trial by military commissions which the British government never recognised, Begg was sent back to the UK in January 2005 by President Bush as a special favour to Prime

Minister Blair. On returning to Britain, Begg was released. He has since published a book and undertaken many interviews where in reasonable terms he refutes all the allegations against him. Yet the US Department of Defense was still insisting in 2006 that Begg 'has strong, long-term ties to terrorism – as a sympathiser, as a recruiter, as a financier and as a combatant'.

The undoubted novelty of a terrorist organisation being able to extend its reach to create such devastation in the two most important American cities led Bush, and Blair too, to claim that this meant that the challenges they now faced were unparalleled in human history. It soon became a feature of the way Bush and Blair spoke after 9/11 that the world they lived in had, almost by definition, to be different from the world past leaders had lived in. Their problems had to be somehow greater and more challenging than those of other leaders – a ludicrous claim when one considers the challenges that the Second World War and the ensuing nuclear weapons confrontation posed for a post-war generation of leaders. The language and rhetoric of both men began to take on the ring of zealotry: nuance and qualification became rarer; certainty and simplicity became ever more dominant.

Bush and Blair liked to pride themselves on being 'big picture' politicians who had the insight to realise that the whole world, not just Afghanistan and Iraq, must now be seen anew and in fundamentally different terms after 2001. In fact, the world, as looked at from the perspective of many centuries, did not change fundamentally on 9/11. There was, however, more irrationality and less predictability. Islamic fundamentalists were ready to sacrifice their lives in committing an act of terrorism, which made bomb-carrying more deadly and a primitive nuclear device in a suitcase conceivable. It took some years for the rhetoric to cool and only in April 2007 did the British government announce formally that it would stop using the term 'war on terror'.

It was to become a feature of both Blair and Bush that neither showed much attention to process or detail, nor were they great respecters of the facts. The combination was, of course, massively unequal in terms of power, but Blair made up for what he lacked in power in the relationship by his far greater verbal fluency and passionate language. Blair's importance was that he reinforced Bush's religious beliefs and prejudices in the period after the invasion of Afghanistan and in the run-up to the war in Iraq. It was a form of what psychiatrists refer to as *folie à deux*. Blair's links with Clinton also helped to keep the Democrats 'on board' for war.

Blair liked Clinton, but he later said to one of his aides, 'Clinton messes you around, but when Bush promises something, he means it.'[24] Experienced officials, however, have questioned whether Blair was deluding himself about his relationship with Bush. They worried about the lack of substance in the Bush–Blair dialogue and about the extent of the mutual posturing. Blair was not Bush's poodle, but he would not take up detailed differences in policy directly with him. Margaret Thatcher had nailed Ronald Reagan down in a way that Blair never did with Bush. John Major, though only having a short time before the 1991 Gulf War period, afterwards built a relationship of some depth with Bush's father.

Blair's own particular form of hubris was his obsession with presentation and his need to put himself visibly at the centre of events. This had already become evident when a private memo he wrote to his staff in 2000 was leaked. In it he urged them to search around for 'two or three eye-catching initiatives . . . I should be personally associated with as much of this as possible'.[25] The biographer of Ramsay MacDonald, another Labour Prime Minister, wrote of Blair's ten years in office:

> The true origin of his tragedy lies in an intellectual deformation that is becoming more and more prevalent in our increasingly paltry public culture. The best word for it is 'presentism' . . . His fascination with fashionable glitz, his crass talk of a 'New Britain' and a 'Young Country' and his disdain for the wisdom of experts who had learned the lessons of the past better than he had were all part of the deadly syndrome.[26]

The world after 9/11 provided Blair with endless opportu-nities for such eye-catching initiatives and he indulged in considerable posturing. Following 9/11 he pursued a frenetic schedule. Over the next few months he held fifty-four meetings with foreign leaders, and travelled more than 40,000 miles on some thirty-one separate flights. Bush, by contrast, was more disciplined than Blair in how he handled his schedule, insisting on having enough time to sleep, and appeared less frenzied and more controlled. The British press were encouraged by No. 10, with its new foreign affairs and defence secretariats, to exaggerate to the British people the extent of the UK's early involvement in Afghanistan. Beyond launching a few Cruise missiles and a contribution from the SAS, the invasion was, first and foremost, an American operation: in all its major parameters it was led by the CIA, who used dollars to build up the Northern Alliance, and by the Pentagon, which used its special forces and air power to tilt the balance of fighting in favour of the Afghan leaders ready to take on the Taleban. But to reinforce the impression of his own central role, Blair flew into Kabul in early January 2002, just eight weeks after the Taleban-controlled capital had fallen to the Northern Alliance, backed by the USA and the UK. He was chronically short of sleep and despite a recent holiday in Egypt was exhausted, mentally and physically.[27] He tried to keep up the same pace through 2002 and much of 2003. Blair's determination to be at the centre of everything was highlighted by the British press. US public opinion, however, liked Blair's easy style, admired his verbal felicity and presentational skills. It suited Bush to build up Blair's importance over Iraq.

By now there was little pretence but that British foreign policy was being run by the Prime Minister from 10 Downing Street, with the Foreign Office being increasingly sidelined. The British Ambassador in Washington recorded this: 'Between 9/11 and the day I retired at the end of February 2003, I had not a single substantive policy discussion on the secure phone with the Foreign Office. This was in contrast to many contacts and discussion with No. 10.'[28]

Blair's hubristic preoccupation with wishing to be seen to be at the centre of events, even if he could achieve nothing of substance, was still present at the G8 meeting in St Petersburg in July 2006. When, unknown to Bush and Blair, a microphone was left switched on, the world was able to hear how the two leaders talked to each other. Bush's 'Yo, Blair!' opening was not reassuring. But what was most revealing was Blair's offer to undertake a piece of shuttle diplomacy over the Lebanon crisis. Blair made it clear that what he had in mind was that he could 'go and just talk' and that a failure on his part to achieve anything would not damage the proposed later visit of Condoleezza Rice, the US Secretary of State. Blair was happy just to act as her advance man. It is not simply that this was demeaning for a British Prime Minister, as was the way Bush inarticulately brushed Blair's offer aside. More particularly it vividly illustrated how Blair's primary focus had become himself, his personal position and its presentation through 'eye-catching initiatives'. This was more important to him now than the substance and complexities of an issue. It remained with him in his restless pursuit of his personal legacy until he left office in 2007. It was still with him in 2012. Unlike Bush, there has been no dignified retirement.

The invasion of Iraq

On the day after 9/11, President Bush said to officials, 'See if Saddam did this. See if he's linked in any way.'[29] It was an odd request to have made since there was very clear evidence that it was al-Qaeda who were responsible for the attacks and Bush had been told this. Al-Qaeda also had a long history of terrorist attacks. In February 1993 the World Trade Center had been singled out: a van bomb filled with 1,500 pounds of urea nitrate was driven into the basement and detonated, killing six people. When Ramzi Yousef, nephew of Khalid Sheikh Mohammed, a key al-Qaeda figure, was captured in Pakistan and later convicted for his part in the attack, police found a mass of newspaper clippings emphasising renown, one of the three Rs already mentioned, as one of the reasons terrorists take such actions.[30]

The US armed forces' presence in Saudi Arabia was highlighted when al-Qaeda killed five American members of a joint military training team there in November 1995.[31] This was followed by the Iranian-backed Hezbollah attacking a residential block outside Riyadh with a suicide truck bomb, killing nineteen Americans. Then a fatwa calling on all Muslims to take part in a jihad to force all US forces to leave Saudi Arabia was announced by Osama bin Laden.

On 7 August 1998 truck bomb attacks organised by al-Qaeda on the American embassies in Nairobi and Dar es Salaam had a horrific impact, to which Clinton responded with Tomahawk missile attacks in Afghanistan and the Sudan. This was followed by a telephone call from a laughing Mullah Omar, the leader of the then Taleban government in Afghanistan, to a senior official in the US State Department.[32]

Less than a month before Bush was elected President, in October 2000, al-Qaeda carried out an attack on the USS *Cole* while in the port of Aden. Furthermore, as long ago as 1995 the Philippine authorities had found a plan, in a laptop computer discovered under a plane seat, to fly aeroplanes into major American buildings such as the World Trade Center. It had been devised by Mohammed Atta, who was to mastermind 9/11. He was captured in Rawalpindi by Pakistan security officials in March 2002, and his interrogation revealed details of 'more than' twenty plots against USA infrastructure targets, including communication nodes, nuclear power plants, dams, bridges and tunnels, which George Tenet, the then head of the CIA, believes would not have been revealed if he had been treated like a white-collar criminal, read his rights and immediately shipped for indictment in New York.[33]

The 9/11 Commission report put an end to scapegoating and hindsight as to whether the Clinton or the Bush administration was responsible for nearly 3,000 people being killed by the al-Qaeda operation. The answer was that both administrations failed.

On 20 September 2001, after 9/11, Blair and Bush met in America and 'when Blair asked about Iraq, the President replied that Iraq was not the immediate problem. Some members of his administration, he commented, had expressed a different view, but he was the one responsible for making the decisions.'[34] We know from Donald Rumsfeld's memoirs published in 2011 that on 26 September, fifteen days after 9/11 Bush asked Rumsfeld to "take a look at the shape of our military plans on Iraq. He knew that the Joint Chiefs and I were concerned about Saddam Hussein's attacks on our aircraft in the northern and southern no-fly zones" . . . and he "wanted the options to be 'creative'." It is easy to forget that between January 2000 and September 2002 Iraq had attacked the US military aircraft enforcing the no-fly zones over Iraq more than two thousand times. [35]

Bush told Rumsfeld on 21 November 2001 to prepare an invasion plan 'and get Tommy Franks [commander in chief of US forces in the Middle East] looking at what it would take'. The Bush administration began publicly and deliberately to link Iraq to al-Qaeda. It also started to convey to the world an image of the USA as a country that would do as it liked and did not need to take other countries into account. International law was treated with contempt. This was Bush's policy every bit as much as that of Rumsfeld and Vice-President Dick Cheney. Bush personally began to show a brash readiness to break out of all international restraints with scant regard for the consequences. By now he was showing many of the signs of hubris syndrome.

In the UK it can be seen how attitudes to a war in Iraq were developing when on 19 July, Jonathan Powell submitted the following well focused memo, copied only to David Manning, on how to handle a phone call to George W Bush.

David Owen

PRIME MINISTER   cc: **David Manning**

IRAQ

We need to give GWB a context for Iraq before he gets his military plan on 4 August. I recommend a phonecall and one of your notes after our meeting next week and before you go on holiday.

I think we need a road map to getting rid of Saddam, drawing parallels as far as possible with his success in Afghanistan, including the following elements:

a) We will be there when the US takes the decision to act, but...

b) We need to set an <u>ultimatum</u> as we did to the Taleban in Afghanistan. At a certain point we need to make it clear that unless Saddam agrees to inspectors on our terms – anyone, anytime, anywhere – by a certain date we will act.

c) We need to establish a <u>legal base</u>. More difficult for us than for them. It needs to be based on WMD rather than terrorism or regime change.

d) We need at least <u>neutrality in the region</u> before we can act. c.f. the effort we put into Pakistan and the Stans before acting in Afghanistan. If we want to base our troops in the region this will mean a real effort on the MEPP (for example difficult to believe Jordan could allow basing without progress).

   We need to devote attention to Turkey – Cyprus, enlargement, political crisis all coming to a head at the same time this autumn.

e) We need to <u>make the case</u>. We need a plan and a timetable for releasing the papers we have prepared on human rights abuses, WMD etc. We need to have the sort of Rolls Royce information campaign we had at the end of Afghanistan before we start in Iraq.

f) We need a <u>convincing military plan</u>. What we know about so far is not convincing. Put the questions our military have.

g) And we need a <u>plan for the day after</u>. Loya Jirga and peacekeeping in Afghanistan have worked well but we had to scramble to get them ready in time. We need to be working on this now for Iraq.

Lastly, we should not rush this. We must do it right. If we are not ready in January 2003 then we may need to wait for autumn 2003. Of course Saddam may give us a break before then that we can exploit, but slow deliberate planning like your father in the Gulf War is the best bet.

This was the background to Blair's thinking when I met him for dinner in Number 10 five days later on 24 July. It then became clear to me that Blair was going to commit Britain to Bush's Iraq policy for while we had another discussion covering the European currency we spent most of the time focusing on Iraq. What was especially noticeable was that, in marked contrast to the way he had previously been ready in December 1998, to explore the complex internal politics of Iraq, Blair was now totally unwilling to have any detailed discussion about the consequences of invading. Even though we both agreed that an invasion was certainly necessary, I felt that the political difficulties certain to be encountered in the aftermath of replacing Saddam and Sunni dominance needed to be explored dispassionately. So I tried to do so in a 'Devil's advocate' manner, but Blair was wholly dismissive. There were no problems that could not be solved and were not being solved.

Blair's purpose in talking to me about Iraq that evening, again with both wives present, was evidently not to consult me but to brief me about what he was going to do and to bring me into the personal 'big tent' of supporters which he liked to create around any controversial new policy. It became utterly clear to me that he had made up his mind on Iraq, and that if Bush later authorised an invasion, Blair would ensure that Britain was there with him, confirmed by Powell's memo "We will be there when the US takes the decision to act". Blair minuted by hand on the memo "I agree with this entirely". I realised that Blair intended me to report from that meeting to my own contacts in the press, on an unattributable basis, that he was definitely going to go to war. This I did as, no doubt, did others. Later, when this readiness to plan for war was eventually confirmed in leaked documents, many people were outraged. But in all fairness, neither Bush nor Blair could indicate their intentions other than by such selective background briefing. It was still months before any invasion could take place. Wars and even the realistic threat of going to war have to be planned for. It takes time, as in the build-up to the Iraq war in 1990–1, to deploy significant armed forces, tanks and heavy weapons. Gradually the British parliament and public knew we were heading for war but that did not mean a final decision had been taken. Rather a path had been set towards war, but one could still stop though it would be harder to do so.

My deep concern about Tony Blair from our meeting was not his support for an invasion, which I shared, nor his wish to get the message out indirectly, which I understood, but the closed nature of his mind. I regret this did not sufficiently alarm me to question him further. I left with the strong impression that Blair was a very different man from the one I had met over dinner in December 1998. Several clear symptoms of hubris syndrome were now manifest that had not been present two and a half years earlier. Besides the messianic belief in his purpose, which was the term my wife used as we discussed the evening driving home, there was a total confidence in himself and a restless, hyperactive manner. His brushing aside of the difficulties that circumstance was likely to throw in his way meant that the die was cast in his own mind over forcing regime change. As before, WMD were not the major topic of conversation, which was focused quite simply on getting rid of Saddam for moral, ethical and geopolitical reasons, all of which I supported.

The opportunity to exercise decisive and controversial leadership is one of the strengths of representative democracy and there is a need from time to time for a certain boldness. But representative democracy also demands that the leader's decision-making be open to democratic scrutiny, that leaders tell the truth to parliament and that those who make the key decisions feel accountable and, if found wanting, are ready to resign from office.

Bush and Blair showed courage in deciding to invade Iraq. Furthermore, I am not attracted to conspiracy theories. I do believe, in contrast to many of their critics, that Bush and Blair thought that gas and chemical weapons were inside Iraq in 2003. So it is claimed did the intelligence services of France, Russia and Israel. I believe Bush and Blair genuinely did fear that these weapons might be used, as gas had been used previously against Iran. They were also concerned about the eventual development of Iraqi nuclear weapons. There was some discussion in Washington and London on whether Iraqi WMD might be passed on to other Muslim countries, although most experts felt this was unlikely given Saddam's suspicion of and hostility towards all his neighbours. But – and it is a big but – both men's strategic aim was regime change, and for perfectly valid reasons. Bush was more open on this. Blair felt he could not be as open.

George Tenet, then head of the CIA, confirms this. 'The United States did not go to war in Iraq solely because of WMD. In my view, I doubt it was even the principal cause. Yet it was the public face that was put on it.'[36]

The nature and the scale of their incompetence was different. In Bush's case it was closely linked to the overconfidence of his close colleagues, Cheney and Rumsfeld. Blair, by contrast, did not have any close ministerial colleagues. The linkage over Iraq between hubris and incompetence has been repeatedly made by a number of serious commentators.[37] But merely asserting the linkage is not sufficient to demonstrate hubris syndrome. There has to be a detailed examination of the nature of each leader's incompetence and of their incoherence which so often accompanies hubris. In addition many straightforward errors of judgement were made. I do not intend to imply by focusing on hubristic incompetence that this was the only cause of error but it was a significant part of the total decision-making.

Hubristic incompetence 1: failure to plan the aftermath

President George W. Bush had two experienced colleagues, Colin Powell and Dick Cheney, who had been his father's principal advisers when Saddam Hussein had invaded Kuwait. A major objective for Saddam then was removing the threat of a $30 billion Kuwaiti debt claim on Iraq. This is why he did not just occupy the disputed Rumailah oilfields but took Kuwait City. He then provocatively went south to the Kuwait–Saudi border, making a direct threat to the Saudis. Right from the start, on 3 August 1990, at the second meeting of the National Security Council with the President, Saddam's personal position was considered. Powell, who was then chairman of the Joint Chiefs of Staff, asked, 'How individualised is this aggression? If he is gone, would he have a more reasonable replacement?' Brent Scowcroft, the National Security Advisor, said, 'Iraq could fall apart,' and a foreign policy specialist, Richard Haas, said, 'It's unlikely that anyone else would have the same cult of personality to hold the country together.'[38]

That conversation remained the basis for the 1991 Desert Storm campaign. The USA would remove Iraqi forces from Kuwait but not attack Baghdad. After midnight on 7 August, Cheney, then Secretary of Defense, saw King Fahd in Jeddah and sought permission to base US forces in Saudi Arabia. He pledged that after the threat was removed, the forces would be withdrawn and the USA would seek no permanent base in the kingdom. The then Crown Prince Abdullah, now the King, spoke against any US forces coming in and reflected the view that such a decision would be very unpopular and that there should be consultation with the tribal elders and religious scholars. King Fahd, very alert to the danger, for the first time in his reign made the decision without a consensus to accept US forces. Insensitive to the domestic debate, the US Air Force asked to base their B52s just 40 miles from the holy city of Mecca.[39]

A substantial multilateral force was assembled by President

George Bush Sr with significant troop contributions from many countries, the largest coming from the UK, France, Saudi Arabia, Egypt and even Syria contributed. On 12 January 1991 Congress voted to authorise the use of force, as did the Senate but in the latter the vote was close: fifty-two to forty-seven. Military success came initially by bombing from the air for six weeks. This was followed on 24 February by a rapid attack with sophisticated tanks, and a large helicopter assault, followed on 27 February by a ceasefire supported by Cheney and Powell. Later Cheney felt it had been a mistake not to eliminate Saddam. But that view has never been shared by the former president, his then Secretary of State James Baker, Scowcroft or Powell.

Against that background, one would have assumed that the question of how to handle in detail the aftermath of another invasion twelve years later would have preoccupied George W. Bush. Yet he appears to have believed simplistically that having toppled Saddam there would be few problems, since the Americans would be seen as liberators. Bush and Blair hubristically and significantly underestimated their enemy, as did General Tommy Franks, who did not take seriously the early signs that Saddam had planned for an insurgency to follow any invasion.[40]

The choice for Bush Jr in 2003 was either a political fix, an early handover and a quick exit, or a programme of nation-building for Iraq, leading to the establishment of a stable democratic government and an exit postponed until this had been achieved. As Commander in Chief Bush should have chosen one or the other of these options before the invasion. What happened was that, sensing division among his advisers, he fatally postponed resolving differences on this issue until well after the invasion. It was clear from their stance on Afghanistan that Cheney and Rumsfeld, well before the invasion of Iraq, were dismissive of the need for nation-building and reluctant to get involved in it. They and the leading neo-conservatives, the deputy Defense Secretary, Paul Wolfowitz, and a colleague at the Department of Defense, Douglas Feith, 'did not believe the US would need to run post-conflict Iraq'. Their aim was to turn the country over very quickly to their favoured Iraqi exiles in the Iraqi National Congress (INC) and make a rapid exit. Late in 2003 Cheney confronted Powell, stuck his finger into his chest and said, 'If you hadn't opposed the INC and Chalabi we wouldn't be in this mess.'[41]

By contrast, the State Department under Powell, favoured nation-building all along. Condoleezza Rice in her memoirs published in 2011, wrote on Bush making light of differences between the departments, "I went to the President and told him that it was an affront to Colin to act that way and we needed the (State Department) expertise. But it was the Defense Department's show and the President was reluctant to intervene." It was a massive error that Bush left this vital issue of aftermath planning unresolved for so long, though he allowed the Cheney–Rumsfeld line initially to gain the upper hand. The Decider failed to decide.

In Britain we know from the subsequent leaking of many

official papers[42] how the aftermath planning issues over Iraq were presented to Tony Blair and how he seems to have ignored the manifest concerns of his officials. For those interested in analysing the mistaken decisions and incompetent execution of British policy, these leaked papers provide a treasure trove of background information. Sir Peter Ricketts, political director of the Foreign Office, warned on 22 March 2002, 'US scrambling to establish a link between Iraq and al-Qaeda is so far frankly unconvincing.'[43] Stories had been emerging of links between al-Qaeda and Iraq and a persistent story in 2001 described how the mastermind of 9/11, Mohammed Atta, had met with an Iraqi intelligence agent at a meeting in Prague five months before the hijacking of the aircraft. I believed this story for a time and wrote about it in the *Wall Street Journal*.[44] But it was wrong and disproved well before the invasion of Iraq. Nevertheless, it was a sign of the loose way intelligence was being used by the White House throughout the war. Lewis 'Scooter' Libby, Cheney's chief aide, was described later by *Time* magazine as responsible for assiduously promoting this very story. *Time* called it a 'hard-to-kill Libby favourite'.[45]

In 2010 Brian Jones, the former head of the UK Defence Intelligence Staff's nuclear, biological and chemical section, published a book called *Failing Intelligence: The True Story of how we were fooled into going to war in Iraq.*[46] He describes how on 3 April 2002 Tony Blair was on his way to Crawford, Texas, and gave an interview to NBC News who asked why he was so concerned about Iraq in terms of its chemical, biological and nuclear weapons. Blair replied "We know that he [Saddam] has stockpiles of major amounts of chemical and biological weapons." Yet Jones writes that the JIC had reported "unequivocally on 15 March in an assessment that went to the Prime Minister that it did not have a clear picture of Iraq's WMD and that any stocks it did have were likely to be small". This was just one example where Blair distorted intelligence information in public, and I wrote formally to Sir John Chilcot, the Chairman of the Iraq Inquiry, to draw attention to this since I was surprised that no evidence appeared to have been taken from Brian Jones. It was formally acknowledged.

All this is not as damning as the charge that the Prime Minister was 'disingenuous'. This arose from a speech that Blair gave in the House of Commons on 24 September 2002 which was first highlighted by Lord Butler in the House of Lords on 22 February 2007. This is described in the conclusion to this book. I also wrote about this to Sir John Chilcot and asked for Lord Butler to be called to explain when he became aware of this and why it had not been highlighted in the inquiry he had earlier chaired. But Butler did not give evidence.

Blair came to a meeting with Bush in Crawford, Texas with clear warnings. The Foreign Secretary, Jack Straw, had written to him on 25 March:

We have also to answer the big question – what will this action achieve? There seems to be a larger hole in this than

71

on anything. Most of the assessments from the US have assumed regime change as a means of eliminating Iraq's WMD threat. *But none has satisfactorily answered how that regime change is to be secured and how there can be any certainty that the replacement regime will be better*[47] (emphasis added).

On 21 July an official's note was circulated to ministers ostensibly on Iraq, titled 'Conditions for Military Action'. It warned:

Little thought has been given to creating the political conditions for military action, *or the aftermath and how to shape it* . . . When the Prime Minister discussed Iraq with President Bush at Crawford in April he said that the UK *would support military action to bring about regime change provided that* certain conditions were met: efforts had been made to construct a coalition, shape public opinion, the Israeli–Palestine Crisis was quiescent, and the options for action to eliminate Iraq's WMD through the UN weapons inspectors had been exhausted . . . *A post-war occupation of Iraq could lead to a protracted and costly nation-building exercise. As already made clear, the US military plans are virtually silent on this point* [48] (all emphasis added).

Two days later Blair was warned about the fixing of intelligence in Washington and was issued an even more serious warning than the one Straw gave in March. A Secret and Strictly Personal 'UK eyes only' memorandum dated 23 July 2002 was eventually leaked to the press two years after the invasion of Iraq and it described a meeting attended by three Cabinet ministers – the Prime Minister, the Foreign Secretary and the Defence Secretary – as well as the Attorney General, but neither Blair's deputy Prime Minister nor the Chancellor of the Exchequer, Gordon Brown, attended. John Scarlett, the head of the JIC, was present, as was the head of MI6, Sir Richard Dearlove, called 'C', who described his recent talks in Washington.

Dearlove reported: 'Military action was now seen as inevitable. Bush wanted to remove Saddam, through military action, justified by the conjunction of terrorism and WMD. But *the intelligence and facts were being fixed around the policy . . . There was little discussion in Washington of the aftermath after military action*[49] (emphasis added). Later Dearlove told George Tenet he had objected to the word 'fixed' in the record of the meeting and had it corrected to reflect his view 'about the undisciplined manner in which the intelligence was being used'. He also said that he had had a polite but significant disagreement with Libby over his belief that there were links between Iraq and al-Qaeda.[50] Also at that meeting was the Chief of the Defence Staff, Admiral Sir Michael Boyce, who said that the military 'were continuing to ask lots of questions. For instance, what were the consequences if Saddam used WMD on day one or if Baghdad did not collapse and urban war fighting began?'[51] Three of Blair's political appointees were also present, Jonathan

Powell, Alastair Campbell and Sally Morgan. Thereafter politics, not military strategy, dominated as they started to prepare public opinion by pushing WMD to the forefront.

What is clear from these leaked papers and my talks with Blair over dinner on 24 July is that the Whitehall machine seemed to be assuming that a protracted and costly nation-building option was likely to be a consequence of any invasion. But, along with the intelligence services, the military were even then deeply alarmed by the lack of any post-invasion planning. Yet Blair was ignoring the warnings his own people were giving him, and in conversation with me at dinner on the very day after the meeting reported above, he was dismissive of any difficulties and tried to give me the impression that it was all being dealt with fully. In this Blair was less than forthright in his dealings with me, a former Foreign Secretary on Privy Council terms, or he was as immune to all my arguments about the problems that might ensue, as he was to much the same arguments being put by people in government. In the end this proved to be the basis for Blair's biggest mistake.

It was pure "wooden-headedness". The very word and characteristic highlighted by the US historian, Barbara Tuchman, in her brilliant book *March of Folly: From Troy to Vietnam*. She wrote that America lost its "virtue" in Vietnam. The first folly was 'continuous overreacting: in the invention of endangered "national security", the invention of "vital interest", the invention of a "commitment", which rapidly assumed a life of its own, casting a spell over the inventor. A second folly was 'illusion of omnipotence'; a third folly was 'wooden-headedness' and the 'Don't-confuse-me-with-the-facts' habit. The US government's 'grossest fault was under-estimation of North Vietnam's commitment to its goal . . . matched by over-estimation of South Vietmam . . . A last folly was the absence of reflective thought.'[52]

That this wooden-headedness remained Blair's frame of mind throughout the autumn of 2002 is confirmed by the experience of Charles Tripp, an academic expert on Middle East politics who was called in along with other experts to give advice. He later wrote an account of his meeting:

At a Downing Street meeting in November 2002 attended by Blair, Straw and six academics familiar with Iraq and the Middle East, two things became clear. The first was that Straw thought post-Saddam Iraq would be much like post-Soviet Russia and could thus be easily pigeon-holed as that strange creature, a 'transitional society'. Either he had been persuaded of this by the recycled Cold Warriors clustering round the Bush administration, or they had failed to inform their 'key ally' of their determination to dismantle Iraq's state and security structures. More ominously, Blair seemed wholly uninterested in Iraq as a complex and puzzling political society, wanting confirmation merely that deposing Saddam would remove 'evil' from the country.[53]

That Blair should be interested only in being reassured that he was fighting evil can be equated with Bush's simple talk of his crusade to rid the world of 'evil doers'.

Unlike in Britain, the unease of the American military about the planning for war was made public. Rumsfeld in his memoirs writes that "in December 2002 the *Washington Post* made headlines with a story that two members of the Joint Chiefs of Staff were opposed to the war in Iraq and to the war plan they had participated in developing, and had approved", namely General Eric K. Shinseki, the US Army Chief of Staff and the Commander of the Marine Corps, General James L. Jones. Rumsfeld wrote "I was astounded by the report, which, if true, deserved the headline it generated." He devotes five pages to the whole saga.[54] "They had each taken part in a number of meetings with the President, with Myers, and with me. Neither Jones nor Shinseki raised concerns either about the wisdom of Bush's intention to go to war if diplomacy failed or of Franks' war plan on how to fight it". Rumsfeld tackled Jones, who, he claimed, apologised and said he was "on board with the plan". Shinseki when tackled, Rumsfeld claims, indicated that the story was not true and asked "who do you believe? The Washington Post or me?"

Six weeks later, however, Shinseki stuck to his guns and told the Senate Armed Services Committee on 25 February 2003, just before the invasion, that, based on his experience of peacekeeping in the Balkans, post-war Iraq would require 'something of the order of several hundred thousand soldiers'.

This was the reasoned estimate of a life-long military man who had lost most of a foot in Vietnam, had led NATO's Peace Stabilization Force in Bosnia, and had commanded both NATO's land forces and the US Army in Europe. The US separation of powers allows for such frankness in Congressional hearings. Traditionally UK service leaders keep their advice to ministers private when appearing before select committees in Parliament. In December 2006 only 141,000 US military personnel were serving in Iraq, together with approximately 16,500 military personnel from twenty-seven coalition partners, the largest contingent being 7,200 from the UK.

The President and Condoleezza Rice, then National Security Advisor, should have insisted on the White House reviewing the planned force levels. Instead Shinseki was contradicted a few days later by Paul Wolfowitz, who told the House Budget Committee that this estimate was 'wildly off the mark', explaining, 'It's hard to conceive that it would take more forces to provide stability in post-Saddam Iraq than it would take to conduct the war itself and to secure the surrender of Saddam's security forces and his army. Hard to imagine.'[55] For those experienced in post-war conflict it was, on the contrary, all too easy to imagine why more forces would be needed in the aftermath. This was particularly the case for the UK military in view of their experience in Northern Ireland over three decades and in Bosnia-Herzegovina from 1992. It is to be hoped that the Iraq Inquiry will reveal what was the advice that Blair was getting from UK Army chiefs about the public debate that went on in Washington about the total number of troops that would be needed in Iraq following the invasion and for how long.

It was also obvious by then it was going to take time to stabilise Afghanistan and if achieved, stability would be very much harder to sustain than in Iraq. Yet when NATO became involved in the Afghan war there was insufficient support from the Western democracies, whether in troop numbers or initially in development aid to build security. The biggest mistake in Afghanistan was to replicate the centralised Western democratic model focused on Kabul when centuries of history showed that only a decentralised model could work. By early 2006 the Taleban were resurgent in the south. The UK did increase its NATO force levels but, again, there was no attempt to warn the British people of the probable consequences. Indeed, Blair's Defence Secretary, John Reid, even implied that troops could come out after three years, having suffered no casualties and not having fired a shot. By contrast, and to its credit, the Dutch government insisted on a long and detailed public debate before it deployed more forces into Afghanistan in 2006. After savage fighting in the south of Afghanistan all through the summer, it was obvious that NATO needed far more troops, helicopters and mobile reserve forces. NATO met in Riga at the end of November 2006 and failed to come up with anywhere near enough extra support, prompting the author of the excellent book, *Jihad: The Rise of Militant Islam in Central Asia*, to write: 'The situation in Afghanistan is not just dire, it is desperate. The struggle against Islamic extremism will be lost not in Iraq, Iran or even the Palestinian territories, but in Afghanistan.'[56] Sadly, at the start of 2012, that prophecy has clearly been proved correct. The fact that Osama bin Laden was found by US forces in Pakistan and killed on 2 May 2011 may help President Obama keep to his announced timetable for withdrawal and make it easier to reach an accommodation with the Taleban but the omens are not good.

In 2002 the US State Department having had its own very detailed aftermath plan for Iraq of around 2,500 pages discarded by the Pentagon, expected that the British Foreign Office would put forward a thoughtful paper on post-invasion planning, in order to restart a dialogue. This was the chance, an experienced Washington commentator thought, for Britain to 'punch above its weight', preferably with Germany and France contributing forces, still a possibility at that stage:

"Britain should have taken the lead. The State Department at least would have regarded a sensible, carefully thought out European initiative as a big assist – especially one on which Britain was out in front and acting as the bridge between America and Europe, which is how London sees its role. In addition, a plan for dealing with post-Saddam Iraq that embodied the thinking and approval of key governments would have had some political heft."[57]

Britain unlike America, had been closely involved in Iraq through most of the twentieth century. By 1918 Britain's Prime

Minister Lloyd George had sent more than a million British and Commonwealth troops into Ottoman territory to impose a post-war settlement.[58] Britain had administered Iraq, albeit not very successfully, under a League of Nations mandate from 1920 until 1932, and had remained close to Nuri al-Said, who dominated the country for the next two decades. It is worth noting that Lloyd George, a successful Prime Minister since 1916, was beginning to develop hubris syndrome when he signed the treaty of Versailles on 28 June 1919. For months after the Paris Conference, he continued to spend an inordinate amount of time hammering out difficult issues in special international conferences. He attended no fewer than thirty-three between 1919 and 1922. The conference habit was summed up in a *Punch* cartoon of that name. He also came to believe he was indispensable. By 1920 Churchill was complaining as War Secretary that the Prime Minister had virtually taken over the running of the Foreign Office and historians have written about these years as the start of a form of presidential government. The two friends did work together over the Anglo-Irish treaty but gradually they drifted further apart than at any other time in their long association. Lloyd George even came close to being contemptuous of Churchill's judgement.[59] In 1922, he was forced out of office by the Conservative MPs, who were the major party in the coalition government.

The knowledge and experience of Iraq in both the British Foreign Office and Ministry of Defence meant they had some well-formulated views on the best way of handling the aftermath of an invasion, especially in the light of the mistakes of 1991. But this expertise was never utilised by Blair and the Foreign Office paper the State Department was hoping for never came. The then British Ambassador to Washington has written about the 'titanic struggle' for six months to keep Britain 'onside for war' and how 'there was little energy left in No. 10 to think about the aftermath. Since Downing Street drove Iraq policy, efforts made by the Foreign Office to engage with the Americans on the aftermath came to nothing.'[60]

This was one of many consequences of Blair taking into his own hands so much of the handling of the preparation for war. The sidelining of the Foreign Office and the Ministry of Defence meant there was little structured Cabinet Committee discussion. Then when Blair met with Bush there was little substantive detailed discussion between them. The normal practice would be for the relevant US and UK Departments to hold prior discussions on all the key issues including dealing with the aftermath. The President and Prime Minister would then focus on any differences that had emerged.

Instead all business of any substance was conducted between the President and Prime Minister and their close confidants and knowledge of those meetings was held very closely within Downing Street.

An example of this is the very restricted circulation of correspondence from Matthew Rycroft at No. 10 to Mark Sedwill, Private Secretary to the Foreign Secretary which shows how resolved the Prime Minister was on taking action in Iraq as early as October 2002, regardless of any second UN resolution. This is a significant piece of evidence which for some reason the Iraq Inquiry did not include in the documents on its website, despite the letter having been made available some time before by the Foreign and Commonwealth Office following a FOI request.

Interestingly, one of the people to whom this letter was copied, Sir Roderic Lyne, at the time HM Ambassador, Moscow, is now a member of the Iraq Inquiry.

Bush and Blair met on 31 January 2003 and some of the leaked detail of that important meeting appeared in a book.[61] But much more detail appeared later in the *New York Times*, their reporter having reviewed a memo of the meeting by the Prime Minister's senior adviser, David Manning, in its entirety.[62] Blair was told that the start date pencilled in for bombing was 10 March 2003. Neither Bush nor Blair seemed to think it necessary to plan for the possible consequences of Bush's own expectation, stated at the meeting, namely that the Iraqi army would 'fold very quickly'. Bush and Blair seemed to envision a quick victory and swapped ideas about the post-war Iraqi government, with Blair saying, 'People would find it very odd if we handed it over to another dictator.' Indeed they would have. Yet both men knew that handing over to US-selected Iraqis was still central to Cheney/Rumsfeld/Wolfowitz thinking. When Blair asked about aftermath planning, 'Condi Rice said that a great deal of work was now in hand.' But Bush still spoke of 'the dilemma' of 'managing the transition to the civil administration', making clear that this issue was still unresolved.

10 DOWNING STREET
LONDON SW1A 2AA

From the Private Secretary

17 October 2002

Dear Mark,

IRAQ: UN ROUTE

The Prime Minister discussed Iraq with the Foreign and Defence Secretaries and CDS on 17 October. Jonathan Powell, Sally Morgan, Alastair Campbell, David Manning and I were also present. **This letter is sensitive. It must be seen only by those with a real need to know its contents, and must not be copied further.**

The Foreign Secretary briefed the Prime Minister on his contacts with Powell and Villepin, and on the latest moves in New York.

The meeting concluded that the only way to keep the US on the UN route was for there to be a clear understanding that if Blix reported an Iraqi breach of the first Resolution then Saddam would not have a second chance. In other words, if for some reason (such as a French or Russian veto) there were no second Resolution agreed in those circumstances, we and the US would take action. At the time the first Resolution was passed, we should make three public points:

(a) When the inspectors returned, Iraq's obligation was not only to cooperate with them on access to sites etc, but also to provide accurate and full information about Iraqi WMD.

(b) If Iraq breached this Resolution, action would follow.

(c) In the meantime, we could not assume a peaceful solution to the problem of Iraq's WMD, so we would outline the military preparations we were making. (It was important to do this only once the Resolution was passed, and not before.)

- 2 -

I am copying this to Peter Watkins (MOD), Ian Fletcher and Desmond Bowen (Cabinet Office), Sir Jeremy Greenstock (UKMis New York), Sir Christopher Meyer (Washington), Sir Roderic Lyne (Moscow), Sir John Holmes (Paris), Sir Nigel Sheinwald (UKRep Brussels) and Sir Emyr Jones Parry (UKDel NATO).

Yours,

[signature]

MATTHEW RYCROFT

Mark Sedwill
FCO

With characteristic hubris, neither man had advisers from defence or foreign affairs ministries in attendance, just their own personal staff from the White House and No. 10. This was the same inner group used to the comfort of recycling together the opinions and prejudices of their respective political masters in frequent exchanges across the Atlantic. What waas developing was a dangerous phenomenon, well documented by management theorists, called 'groupthink'. Described as a 'personality-determined malaise', the symptoms of this process are well described in the book *On the Psychology of Military Incompetence*[63] and were displayed in President Kennedy's handling of the Bay of Pigs fiasco on coming into office in the spring of 1961. Past military incompetence produces four most frequently occurring symptoms: 'wastage of manpower, over-confidence, underestimation of the enemy and the ignoring of intelligence reports'.

Blair's final meeting with Bush before the war was in the Azores in the middle of March, with the Prime Ministers of Spain and Portugal present.

All Blair says in his memoirs of what happened at that meeting is "it was a slightly surreal event. On the face of it, we were still pushing for a political solution. There were some last-minute hopes of an Arab initiative to get Saddam out; or of a Saddam capitulation . . . we rehearsed again the main argument. He (Bush) was completely calm. He thought we had to send out a message of total clarity to the world: have anything to do with WMD and we are going to come after you. More even than me, he was focused on the possibility of terrorist groups getting hold of WMD material."[64]

As Condoleezza Rice makes clear in her memoirs Blair had to return for a debate in the House of Commons two days later, and as they said goodbye she said to Bush's Chief of Staff, "I hope it's not the last time we see them." This was a sign of melodramatic spin on the result (of the debate) which was never in doubt since there was strong support from the Conservative party. The only question was the size of the Labour revolt. In the event it was smaller than anticipated.

So Bush and Blair committed their troops to war with no idea as to how long they would remain an occupying force. As one former covert CIA man put it:

> There was no question we'd get to Baghdad in no time. We better have a plan for when we get there. But we had nothing but four PowerPoint pages. It was arrogant. We used to joke about the PhD club – Wolfowitz, Feith. They knew best . . . We set the conditions for how that happened. This is a self-inflicted mess.[65]

It also meant that one of Henry Kissinger's three conditions for war in Iraq, heard by the UK Ambassador in July 2002, had not been fulfilled. Kissinger said the USA had to 'arrive in Baghdad with a clear plan for the succession to Saddam. It would be disastrous to begin debating a successor regime after deposing him'.[66]

On 17 January 2003 a retired lieutenant general, Jay Garner, was asked by Douglas Feith to take charge of post-war Iraq and formed the Office of Reconstruction and Humanitarian Assistance. He was given no existing plans. Feith hoped Garner would turn to Ahmed Chalabi and his band of exiles.[67] At their meeting on 31 January 2003, Bush and Blair had grandly declared that 'failure was not an option'. But both men had already sown the seeds of their combined failure before the invasion started. Brave leaders often sweep cautious advice aside but it was foolhardy for Bush and Blair not to realise that the concerns that had been expressed to them had substance. Not to plan to prevent those concerns materialising was reckless; indeed, it was more than reckless – it was a culpable dereliction of duty. The handling, or rather the non-handling, of the vital issues of planning beforehand and what to do with an occupied Iraq, and also to fail to provide sufficient troops to maintain order, constituted a piece of hubristic incompetence on the part of Bush and Blair which has brought nemesis on hundreds of thousands of people. Their responsibility is manifest – it cannot be shifted on to their subordinates or on to the Iraqis.

In her memoirs, Condoleezza Rice admits to failure. "On the issue of rear-area security, . . . I failed to get a workable plan for the President. That turned out to be a big problem in the days immediately following Saddam's overthrow. As our forces pushed through, chaos ensued behind them. Neither we nor the British had enough troops to keep order."

In the event it was only after the momentum of a successful invasion was lost that Bush and Rice focused on the detailed arrangements for the transition. Paul Bremer arrived in Baghdad in May 2003 as the American head of the Coalition Provisional Authority with the powers of a viceroy, insisting on reporting to Bush. It had been decided to hold off on Garner's public promise of elections within ninety days and an early transfer of sovereignty. Part of the process was to sideline and eventually diminish Chalabi's influence. So the nation-building option was, in effect, adopted by Bush but with far too few troops to make it workable, particularly since an insurgency was underway.

Bush, in his memoirs, quite unlike Blair, admits to error in the conduct of war in Iraq in forthright terms. "The first is that we did not respond more quickly or aggressively when the security situation started to deteriorate after Saddam's regime fell. In the ten months following the invasion, we cut troop levels from 192,000 to 109,000. Many of the remaining troops focused on training the Iraqi army and police, not protecting the Iraqi people. We worried we would create resentment by looking like occupiers. We believed we could train Iraqi security forces to lead the fight. And we thought progress toward a representative democracy, giving Iraqis of all backgrounds a stake in their country, was the best path to lasting security. While there was logic behind these assumptions, the Iraqi people's desire for security trumped their aversion to occupation. Cutting troop levels too quickly was the most important failure of execution in the war."[68]

Hubristic incompetence 2: Blair's pursuit of a second UN resolution

Seven months before the invasion of Iraq it was the US Secretary of State, Colin Powell, who persuaded George W. Bush, correctly, to go first to the UN before embarking on direct military intervention. Powell warned Bush, over dinner on 5 August 2002, 'A war with Iraq could be much more complicated and bloody than the war in Afghanistan,' as American unilateral intervention was not possible. According to the journalist Bob

Woodward, Powell said, 'You can still make a pitch for a coalition or UN action to do what needs to be done,' and he warned of a 'cauldron' in the Arab world that 'would suck the oxygen out of just about everything else the United States was doing, not only in the war on terrorism, but all other diplomatic, defence and intelligence relationships'.[69] On going to the UN, Powell's arguments were strongly reinforced by Tony Blair. On 12 September, with the crucial paragraph missing from his script, Bush ad-libbed in his UN General Assembly speech that the USA would work with the UN Security Council for the necessary resolutions but had meant to say 'resolution' in the singular. The French seized on this verbal infelicity to push for two resolutions but the Americans never conceded this. On 11 October the US Senate authorised the use of the armed forces, by seventy-seven votes to twenty-three, against Iraq. The President was free to take action as 'he determines to be necessary and appropriate'.

The unanimous passing in the Security Council of Resolution 1441 on 8 November 2002 was a diplomatic feat, but it was also a political fudge. France, Germany and Russia were still far from being convinced of the case for invading Iraq. The wording of the resolution, however, succeeded in putting increased international pressure on Saddam Hussein and made military action more likely if he did not comply. The extent of the US diplomatic success can be measured by the response of the French. By 9 December there had developed 'a seeming harmony between the US and French viewpoints'.[70] A French general went to Washington on 21 December to offer between 10,000 and 15,000 troops and 100 aircraft to deploy after the UN Chief Inspector's first report, due on 27 January 2003, which the French expected to be unfavourable to Saddam. On 13 January, President Chirac sent a personal envoy to speak to Rice with the French ambassador, Jean-David Levitte, who had been at the UN during the negotiations over Resolution 1441. They said they did not want to veto a second resolution and therefore they would prefer the USA to go to war just on Resolution 1441, if the USA felt diplomacy was over.

In the immediate aftermath of the unanimous vote in the Security Council, and with Bush enjoying overwhelming support in Congress, it would have been wiser for Blair to have already made clear to Parliament that Resolution 1441 could be enforced on WMD only if Saddam were removed. The reason why this would have been sensible is that it would have enabled Blair openly to make the very important connection between advocating the deposing of Saddam as necessary regime change, in order to enforce compliance with resolutions requiring the removal of WMD. Regime change could never attract sufficient support within the UN as an objective in itself but by connecting the two it could have won additional support in the UN and would certainly have widened public support and understanding in Parliament.

The interpretation of the UN Charter is the responsibility of the Security Council, which is not a court of law but a collection of member states empowered to act under their interpretation of the charter. Lawyers' advice is but one of many factors to weigh in the balance when negotiating the terms of a UN resolution. Probably the most succinct and authoritative criticism of the legality of the UK Government's military action in Iraq came from the late Lord Bingham, a very distinguished Lord Chief Justice. "If I am right that the invasion of Iraq by the US, the UK and some other states was unauthorised by the Security Council there was, of course, a serious violation of the international law and of the rule of law. For the effect of acting unilaterally was to undermine the foundation on which the post-1945 consensus had been constructed: the prohibition of force (save in self defence, or, perhaps, to avert an impending humanitarian catastrophe) unless formally authorised by the nations of the world empowered to make collective decisions in the Security Council under Chapter VII of the UN Charter. The moment that a state treats the rules of international law as binding on others but not on itself, the compact on which the law rests is broken. "It is", as has been said, "the difference between the role of world policemen and world vigilante."[71] His viewpoint rests on whether or not it was unauthorised and I discuss this again in the concluding chapter on legal evidence made available to the Iraq Inquiry.

Demanding the resignation of a head of government by UN Security Council resolution under threat of action, in the terms of Chapter VII of the charter, can be justified as an action taken to overcome an already existing threat to the peace. A threat to the peace overrides the charter's injunction not to interfere in another state's internal sovereignty. Only after 9/11 did such a demand become a practical option in Iraq because of a readiness in the USA to invade rather than continue with enforcing the no-fly zone. Demanding that Saddam step down from power, in order to ensure the removal of all possibility of Iraq developing WMD, with a UN-supervised election to choose a successor, could have been Bush and Blair's first diplomatic response in 2002, followed if the resolution was vetoed by a threat of invasion. This would have been far better than focusing on WMD alone and could have been justified by Saddam's long record of flouting UN existing resolutions.

Arguing the necessity of removing Saddam in order to enforce UN resolutions on WMD would have helped Blair with the Labour Party. It would also have had a further benefit: the British military could have been openly involved in detailed planning of the invasion and its aftermath months in advance. Instead Blair held back on involvement. A Britain involved fully would have been in a stronger position to argue in Washington for larger numbers of troops to be deployed in the aftermath to stabilise the country, control its borders and prevent an insurgency. The USA and the UK military collaboration started earlier over the first Gulf War of 1991, with British military involvement right from the start of planning in the autumn of 1990. Moreover, a British general with much Arab experience, Sir Peter de la Billière, was hugely influential as Deputy Commander under General Norman Schwarzkopf.

The greatest benefit, by far, however, of earlier involvement would have been that Parliament and the British people would have been told the truth. Britain was going to war for the combined purpose of getting rid of Saddam and in order to guarantee that this time, unlike in 1991, WMD, if they existed, would be forcibly removed never to return. And with Saddam removed from power, all UN resolutions would be fully implemented within months.

Blair became fixed instead on the need to secure a second Security Council resolution explicitly authorising the resort to war. His belief that he could get such a resolution passed showed extraordinary blindness and a dismissive contempt for those who warned him he could not succeed. In part he appears to have deluded himself about his own powers of persuasion. His pursuit of the second resolution also demonstrated an astonishing disregard for the damage it would cause to the carefully crafted consensus that had been achieved through the unanimous passing of Resolution 1441. In addition Blair's stance meant compromises offered by the French were not pursued. In short, his conduct over the chimera of a second resolution manifested a monumental misjudgement born out of hubris.

Why did Blair want a second resolution? The case for Resolution 1441 alone providing sufficient legality for going to war rested on the legal claim that it revived Resolutions 678 and 687, going back to the first Gulf War, which themselves countenanced the use of military force. This was a controversial interpretation which some in the UK disputed. In the Security Council itself there were always different interpretations of

Resolution 1441, as there had been in relation to the other UN resolutions on Iraq in the 1990s. Also while it was undisputed that Resolution 1441 required the Security Council to meet before the start of any military action, there was an argument as to whether it needed expressly to confirm 'material breach by Iraq' of earlier resolutions or to pass another resolution specifically endorsing military action. For the USA, and to a slightly lesser extent for the UK, there was a commitment only to meet 'in order to consider the situation and the need for full compliance with all of the relevant Council Resolutions in order to secure international peace and security'. America was firm that a further decision of the Security Council was not required by the terms of Resolution 1441, taken with the entire series of earlier Security Council resolutions requiring Iraq to disarm. Ambiguity over interpretation was not an accident, nor is it uncommon in the Security Council: it was part of the political reality and the compromises which had enabled the unanimous passing of Security Council Resolution 1441 to be negotiated in the first place.

So to those familiar with the workings of the Security Council, in America and in Britain, it was somewhat surprising, to say the least, that Blair was now pushing so hard for a second resolution which he was unlikely to achieve. Cheney and Rumsfeld were predictably totally against the attempt and even Colin Powell was only supportive because he felt Blair needed it politically. Powell had been told by Bush on 13 January that the USA was going to invade. On 19 January, Bush, privately and reluctantly, accepted Blair's passionate plea for a second UN resolution. American lack of enthusiasm was understandable because they knew the French were still ready to compromise. Then at a press conference on 20 January, the French Foreign Minister, Dominique de Villepin, provocatively and flamboyantly declared 'Nothing! Nothing!' justified war. This was after he became convinced, having met Powell on the 19th, that war was inevitable. On the 21st, Jean-David Levitte again made representations to the Americans. He appeared to want to pull back from Villepin's exposed position the previous day. He was unlikely to have done this entirely on his own initiative. The French ambassador in London, however, undertook no similar exercise. Levitte suggested that France and the USA should agree as friends to disagree. If there was to be a war, France would reluctantly acquiesce in any military action taken under Resolution 1441. They would not themselves send troops, but they would not actively support any condemnatory UN resolution of such action, provided that they would not face a second resolution. There was every reason to believe that Russia and China would abstain on such a deal and Germany would acquiesce. In the meeting Levitte was given no encouragement by the USA to think that it would drop the second resolution.

It was not unambiguously the case that the Security Council had to pass another resolution therefore authorising war for such a war to be claimed to be legal. Blair's privately stated view, at his 31 January 2003 meeting with Bush, was that a second Security Council resolution would provide an 'insurance policy'.[72] Why, then, did Blair want this insurance policy? Partly perhaps because he knew he had not been honest about regime change to the British public and that he was overstressing WMD to overcome the strong dissent within the Labour Party about the legality of going to war solely on the basis of 1441. Naturally any Prime Minister would want to win the support of his party for war and politically it was desirable for Blair to carry Parliament's endorsement on Labour Party votes alone. But to carry one's own MPs is not essential for parliamentary authority. Blair was content later to carry through important education reforms on Conservative votes, and arguably even in the debate on the replacement for the Trident nuclear deterrent on 14 March 2007. The Conservative opposition in 2003 was steadfastly in favour of the US over Iraq, so Parliament's overall support for the war was never in doubt and parliamentary authority for military action, if sought, on Resolution 1441 was always going to be given.

But in the attempt primarily to obtain the votes of more Labour MPs, Blair was pitching himself against hopeless odds and risking almost certain defeat in the Security Council in trying to get a second resolution passed. Furthermore, by so determinedly pursuing it he risked undermining the credibility of the claim that existing resolutions provided legal cover for war. For if that was the case, his critics would, and did, say, why would there need to be all this effort to get a second resolution? The explanation for Blair's stance was in part, once again, hubris.

Bush, after meeting Blair, very noticeably gave only a

lukewarm public endorsement of a second resolution, with Blair alongside him at their 31 January press conference in Washington.[73] It is now clear why. For even as Blair was publicly insisting on the importance of a second resolution Bush himself had just been privately told by Blair that he only regarded it as an insurance policy. In the leaked memo written by Blair's adviser David Manning, recording that meeting on 31 January 2003, the whole flavour of the discussion between Bush and Blair is one of cynicism over the second resolution still being pursued. Bush is quoted as saying he was determined to invade Iraq and that *military action would follow anyway* (emphasis added) even without the second resolution and even if international arms inspectors failed to find WMD. Blair replied that he was 'solidly with the President and ready to do whatever it took to disarm Saddam'. So the second resolution he was pursuing at such risk to the whole strategy did not ultimately matter to him anyway. It is another example of contempt being at the heart of hubris.

At that same meeting Bush offered Blair the opportunity for them to combine Resolution 1441 with regime change. Bush said, 'At some point, probably when we had passed the second resolution – assuming we did – we should warn Saddam that he had a week to leave. We should then notify the media too. We would then have a clear field if Saddam refused to go.'[74] For some reason not yet explained this issue was never taken up in this form, but it would have been a dramatic way of focusing on regime change and certainly of making it clear before the invasion that WMD and regime change went together. At the meeting Bush unwisely predicted that it was 'unlikely there would be internecine warfare between the different religious and ethnic groups' and Blair agreed with that assessment. It was yet another sign of how out of touch both leaders had become.

In Washington, as Bob Woodward reported, some were not keen to take any French offer to compromise; they thought a clash with France would be a 'liberating moment for the United States and even more so for Prime Minister Blair . . . the whole UN process was hopeless. Bush and Blair could argue that they had gone to the UN and been thwarted by the French.'[75] But it proved not to be a liberation for Blair but a humiliation. By persisting in the belief he could secure the necessary votes for a second resolution and not picking up on the French compromise, Blair demonstrated hubristic inflexibility. The votes were not there in the UN for a second resolution and Blair was told this. But he ignored that advice. He obviously did not trust President Chirac, who had warned him in October that 'while Saddam Hussein could be overthrown, the subsequent conse-quences would be disastrous'.[76] Blair had also discussed Iraq with Chirac over a long period, and he saw him as protecting France's economic links with Iraq. It is unclear if the French offer to abstain in the Security Council was ever discussed by the UK Cabinet or a smaller number of ministers. We have yet to see any evidence made public whether Blair ever used Britain's diplomatic links and particularly the previously established Quadripartite mechanism in order to try to bring France and

Germany back into a *modus vivendi* with the USA and the UK over the invasion.

This was the time for compromise among the four foreign ministers, from the USA, the UK, France and Germany; the Quadripartite countries had a long history of quietly working out much more difficult questions, originally over Berlin, but also on many other serious areas of foreign and security policy, and in particular on reaching agreement over wars. Quadripartite had, however, progressively lost its clout; some date the start of this to the 1996 Berlin negotiations, when the Americans felt that the European three – Britain, France and Germany – had ganged up on them over EU access to NATO assets. Eventually an agreement was concluded in 2002 as the Berlin Plus Agreement. Quadripartite was, however, the ideal forum for resolving the growing divisions over Iraq. An agreement, along the lines which the French proposed, to stick with Resolution 1441 would have demonstrated the all-important truth that the Security Council is a political forum, not a court of law.

Blair's problem with such diplomacy was that it would have meant involving others, particularly his own Foreign Secretary, as well as the other Quadripartite foreign ministers. That process, I suspect he felt, would have diminished his own hands-on involvement. He preferred to pursue his high-profile arm-twisting exercise on the French and other Security Council members. He therefore pressed on with the pursuit of a second resolution, simply ignoring the French warning that they had already secured the blocking majority of nine votes against the UK and US position in the Security Council. We still do not yet know from the Iraq Inquiry whether the UN department, now called the International Organizations Department, in the Foreign Office, as distinct from the UK's permanent representative at the UN, ever produced a written professional assessment about the true state of the likely Security Council voting or whether, if it did, it was ever read in Downing Street. Among the key purposes of the UN department in the past has been to weigh the views on UN resolutions in the capitals of the fifteen Security Council countries, to test the UK permanent representative's view from New York and to advise the Foreign Secretary and through him or her the Cabinet. If such a professional assessment was written, it is hard to believe that it could have endorsed Blair's belief that a second resolution was winnable. The Inquiry will hopefully focus on this.

The Americans attempted to win around the doubtful members of the Security Council with the British. But Dominique de Villepin went further across the frontier of friendship with his UK and US colleagues and toured Africa, cajoling Security Council members to vote against the second resolution. Buoyed up by the fervour of the moment, Blair failed to pick up in No. 10 that the British initiative was unravelling in New York. Not since Anthony Eden and Suez has a British Prime Minister so misjudged the mood of the Security Council. Eventually, on 8 March, it became apparent even to No. 10 that the French had counted their votes more precisely all along and that the six undecided countries (Pakistan, Cameroon, Angola, Guinea, Chile and Mexico) would not support the second resolution. With a derisory level of support, it had to be dropped.

Sir Stephen Wall, the diplomat inside No. 10 in charge of Blair's relationship with the EU, recalled the moment when, with his press secretary, Blair split the EU asunder. 'I happened to be in the corridor in No. 10 when he and Alastair Campbell were walking down the corridor and they decided effectively to play the anti-French card.'[77] They ignored that Chirac's threat to use the veto was only stated for that evening, '*ce soir*', and they played on incipient British anti-French feeling. It was naked politics but both felt it would help carry the day in Parliament.

The French position was not a principled one. Villepin wobbled as he played to the gallery of world opinion in January and February. He believed that France could hold out only until the middle of March and would then have to support the USA. That position was changed by Chirac in February but the President had also been hedging his bets in December and January. Hence the reasonable conclusion that 'France's govern - ment was not so much struggling to save humanity as looking out for Numéro Un'.[78]

Over the second resolution, Blair's failure to achieve a goal the pursuit of which had always been vain (in both senses of the word) proved hugely costly. Not only did the effort itself undermine the credibility of the claim, which ultimately had to be relied on, that the invasion was legal without a second resolution, but the futile process shattered what consensus had been achieved over Resolution 1441 and sharpened the divisions within the international community. It also exacerbated the splits between the EU countries on the Security Council, with the French rallying opposition to the resolution while the Spanish and British were shown as incompetent. So much for all Blair's pro-EU rhetoric.

The fiasco over pursuing the second resolution was very much Blair's own. He clearly had delusions about his own capacity to succeed. He was contemptuous of the advice and warnings of others. He rejected a sensible compromise when it was offered. He persisted in spite of reality staring him in the face. And he was utterly cavalier about the risks he was running and the likely costs of failure.

Blair's manipulation of international law and intelligence

On 7 March 2003 Lord Goldsmith, the Attorney General and constitutionally the government's independent legal adviser, sent Tony Blair a memo titled 'Advice on the Legality of Military Action against Iraq without a Further Security Council Resolution'.[79] It was a long, balanced judgment but in places it was clearly equivocal. It said that a 'reasonable case' could be made that Resolution 1441 could 'in principle' revive the authorisation to attack Iraq but admitted that such a case would be challengeable in court. As usual, this advice was not made public but nor was it shown to the Cabinet.

The Chief of the Defence Staff, Admiral Sir Michael Boyce, who all along was clearly concerned about the legal position and demanded unequivocal reassurance from the Attorney General about the legality of the action to which he was about to commit troops. This was against the background of disquiet about the creation of the new International Criminal Court (ICC), and the alleged risk that UK service personnel might be indicted by that court for their conduct during the war. In fact, the ICC cannot prosecute an illegal war, known as a crime of aggression, for its 'jurisdiction is limited to the conduct of war, not the decision to go to war'.[80] The subsequent occupation and reconstruction in Iraq were later authorised by the Security Council, though on the basis that this authority did not extend to the original military intervention.

On 17 March Goldsmith produced a very much shorter and unequivocal statement which said that 'a material breach of Resolution 678 revived the authority to use force under Resolution 678'. This statement was given orally to the Cabinet and reiterated in Parliament. It was claimed by Blair that the second statement was merely an abbreviated version of the first and he resisted all attempts for the first to be published. In response to the continuing controversy, almost exactly two years later, on 9 March 2005, Blair said, 'It is being said that the legal opinion of the Attorney General was different from the Attorney General's statement to the House. That is patently absurd.' Yet the Information Commissioner, Richard Thomas, served an enforcement notice in 2006 on the Attorney General, requiring a disclosure statement because Goldsmith's advice on 7 March 2003 was 'significantly more equivocal' than his statement on 17 March. The disclosure statement was published on 26 May 2006. The Attorney General's first formal legal opinion was, to any fair-minded person, long, equivocal in places, but balanced. The second was short and unambiguous in its judgment. The Cabinet should undoubtedly have been made aware of the risks of a future legal challenge. Yet Blair, in his memoirs, says that in the Cabinet discussion on Monday 17 March the then Lord Chancellor "Derry Irvine came in with a very helpful intervention saying that if France had not threatened to veto any resolution authorising action, we could probably have got a second resolution and the problem was we tried so hard to get a second resolution people assumed, wrongly, we needed one legally."[81] A perceptive political commentator in *The Times*, commenting on Tony Blair's mental state, referred to him as 'unhinged', in the serious sense of the word, as early as 29 March 2003 and went on to cite his throwaway remark in Parliament that he would ignore Security Council vetoes which were 'capricious' or 'unreasonable'.

What is more troubling is Blair's description eight years later of his mental state at the time when leaving the Azores. "I knew the die was cast. I was aware of my isolation, my precarious grip on power, and – stomach-churning thought – my total dependence on things going right not wrong. What's more, this was the first time I would be committing ground troops to action to topple a regime where we would be the junior partner, where we would not be in charge of all the arrangements." [82]

The facts are very different. In Kosovo where his hubris began to emerge he was not in charge of all the arrangements. This was a humanitarian intervention by NATO. The Supreme Allied Commander in Europe was in charge of the operation and the American armed forces made by far the largest contribution flying some 62% of the total sorties over the 78-day air campaign compared to the UK's 10 per cent.[83] Yet to read Blair's account in his memoirs of the Kosovo campaign is to realise how totally self-centred and even deluded it still was in 2011.[84] No explanation is given as to why his government initially ruled out the threat of ground forces and castigated those who advocated it. No recognition of President Yeltsin's contribution in demanding that Milosevic should order the Serbian military to withdraw. Everything depended, so Blair seems to believe, on the pressure he applied to Bill Clinton to contemplate using ground forces. In reality, the decisive event, on 14 April was Yeltsin's appointment of his former Prime Minister, Victor Chernomyrdin (and importantly the former head of Gazprom, since Serbia was hugely dependent on Russian gas), to be his special envoy for dealing with Kosovo. The subsequent turbulent diplomacy is engagingly described by Strobe Talbott[85] in a chapter called "The Hammer and the Anvil" where Chernomyrdin was the hammer and Ahtisaari, the Finnish President, the anvil. Talbott, Russian speaking and a close friend of Clinton since student days, proved to be the modest but irreplaceable facilitator. The Russians have never revealed their negotiating hand but it is highly probable that Milosevic only ordered his senior military officers on 3 June to withdraw from Kosovo when on an earlier visit to Belgrade, he was told quite specifically by Chernomyrdin that there would be no more Russian gas if he did not do so.

Whatever the controversy about the war in Iraq it is only fair to recognise that Tony Blair and Jack Straw took the issue to the House of Commons on Tuesday 18 March. Blair delivered a remarkably effective speech and won the support of MPs on a cross party basis by 412 to 149 votes. It was a democratic decision and it was one that I supported.

It was widely believed that Blair had leaned on his political appointee, the Attorney General, to change his legal advice, although Goldsmith has strenuously denied this. A senior Foreign Office lawyer resigned in protest as the war began. Whether or not it is true that Blair manipulated his own Attorney General, it is undoubtedly the case that Blair broke the Ministerial Code of Conduct by denying his Cabinet access to the full, written advice, as the code requires. But Blair's manipulation of the Cabinet was not new. It had been occurring for more than five years on domestic issues as well as inter - national issues. But it was getting worse.

Even more hubristic was the way, before the invasion, both Blair and George W. Bush were prepared to manipulate intelligence information to suit their ends. On WMD both leaders presented it as being definitive when in fact it was often nuanced and tentative. Blair personally made significant errors in stressing, when the CIA was unsure, the intelligence from the Italians that uranium oxide or 'yellow cake' was ready to be shipped to Iraq from Niger. Blair was also wrong to allow the claim of only a 45-minute warning of an Iraqi missile firing to be hyped up or as the BBC reporter described the process - "sexed up". The missiles were known to be only short range and unable to hit such targets, but nevertheless No. 10 briefed the tabloid newspapers, who reported prominently, one on the front page, that this would mean virtually no warning of attacks against British forces in Cyprus and the Middle East. When reporting to Parliament and explaining privately to colleagues, Blair stripped out too many of the caveats that MI6's innate caution had added. In fairness to Blair, Lord Hutton's report found the intelligence had not been 'sexed up'. Many people who studied the proceedings of the Hutton inquiry came to a different conclusion, based on reading much of the same evidence.

Politicians down the ages have presented their side of any case in the best possible light, focusing on what is positive and ignoring the negative. Political spin, as it is called, did not start with Bush and Blair. What was new about these two was their readiness to spin intelligence matters. Their 'spinmasters', in the shape of Karl Rove and Alastair Campbell, were not only more powerful than similar figures in the past but they were uniquely deeply involved in the domestic debate about Iraq and themselves briefed on intelligence matters. In Blair's case,

Campbell was involved in the publication of two dossiers purportedly outlining the threat posed by Saddam. One of them, which came to be known as 'the dodgy dossier', was derided by the Foreign Secretary, Jack Straw, as a 'horlicks' and was withdrawn by the government itself; the other was widely believed to have used tentative intelligence assessments in order to make a compelling propaganda case in favour of war. One Cabinet minister, the former Foreign Secretary, the late Robin Cook, questioned the validity of the interpretation being put on intelligence information and wisely asked for – and received – a personal briefing from MI6. He then resigned and voted against the invasion of Iraq, saying in the House of Commons that he did not believe the intelligence justified it. In fairness to his judgement, the intelligence briefing notes prepared for him should now at least be seen by the Iraq Inquiry panel, for them to draw their own conclusions. Also Charles Kennedy, then leader of the Liberal Democratic Party, urged his party to vote against the whole venture. The vote in Parliament of Labour MPs on their own gave Blair a majority. But it was all gained at a bitter price in terms of broken trust.

Blair had enjoyed considerable trust from almost all sides of the political spectrum in Parliament until the point came when his manipulation of the facts gravely damaged that trust. As those facts became better known, Blair's name began to be defaced to 'Bliar' and he could no longer rely on the automatic support that the British Parliament and people traditionally give to a Prime Minister in a time of war.

After the invasion

Revealingly, an American book on the Iraq War was simply called *Hubris*.[86] On 1 May 2003, George W. Bush, dressed like a Hollywood actor in flying gear, flew onto the aircraft carrier *Abraham Lincoln* off the coast of California and stood on the flight deck to celebrate victory in Iraq, the ship's control tower emblazoned with the slogan 'Mission Accomplished'. It was a hubristic act of a very high order. It was also a contemptuous, if unintended, insult to the troops in the field, who knew all too well the slogan's patent absurdity. Donald Rumsfeld had the sense to dissuade Bush from actually using the phrase in his speech but even so Bush did say, 'In the battle for Iraq, the United States and our allies have prevailed.' Tony Blair never went so far but his early rhetoric was also far too triumphant.

Rumsfeld, in response to the rapid breakdown of law and order in Baghdad and widespread looting, most of which was the result of Bush accepting his advice that there were sufficient troop numbers on the ground to control the occupation simply said, 'Stuff happens.' It took a playwright, David Hare, to dramatise the deeper significance of this remark.[87]

The scale of incompetence after the invasion of Iraq will be something over which historians will long puzzle. How could Washington, particularly the Pentagon, be so incompetent on both the political and military organisational levels? One answer lies in the aloofness and indifference to detail of the Commander in Chief, to which many witnesses of Bush's behaviour testify. A candid assessment of these characteristics in Bush's conduct in office came from a former Secretary of the Treasury, Paul O'Neill, who served from 2000 until 2002. He comments that from the start Bush was 'clearly signing on to strong ideological positions that had not been fully thought through. But of course, that's the nature of ideology. Thinking it through is the last thing an ideologue wants to do.' O'Neill goes on to describe one meeting as 'like many of the meetings I would go to over the course of two years. The only way I can describe it is that, well, the President is like a blind man in a roomful of deaf people. There is no discernible connection.'[88]

Another example involved David Kay, the former UN weapons inspector in Iraq, who since 5 June 2003 had been given the task of finding WMD. He was at Bush's early morning briefing on 29 July, having flown in from Baghdad the day before. He told the President: 'The biggest mistake we made was to let looting and lawlessness break out,' and he went on to warn that they had not found any WMD and might not find any. Kay left the meeting almost shocked at Bush's lack of inquisitiveness on WMD, especially when compared with Dick Cheney's detailed probing.[89] Looters, by then, had taken two tons of unprocessed uranium, 'yellow cake', 194 tons of high-melting-point explosives and 141 tons of rapid detonation explosives.[90]

Bush discussed 'de-Ba'athification' on 10 March before the invasion and was told only one to two per cent of the 25,000 members of the party were active. While the conclusions lacked specificity, one person at the meeting has since said, 'The thrust was clear: treat these people leniently and try to work with them.'[91] But what was extraordinary was that the eventual document forcing de-Ba'athification, issued by Paul Bremer, brought in to head up the American effort in Iraq, was shown neither to Condoleezza Rice nor to Colin Powell, who believed the policy drafted in Douglas Feith's office did not represent the compromise the war cabinet had agreed on 12 March. That agreement was for the preservation of three to five army divisions that would form the nucleus of a new Iraqi army. It was a fateful mistake by Rice to allow this to go out from Bremer without it being checked. The British Secretary of State for Defence, Geoff Hoon, said in May 2007 that to de-Ba'athify was an error. 'I think we felt that a lot of the Ba'ath people were, first and foremost, local government people and, first and foremost, civil servants – they weren't fanatical supporters of Saddam.'[92]

Bremer's vice-regal style was epitomised by the formal order, which he issued eleven days after arriving in Iraq, in which he dissolved the Iraqi army, air force, navy, ministry of defence and intelligence services. Bremer had not consulted the State Department, the CIA or Rice on the terms of the order, nor did he mention it to Iraqi politicians. This was perhaps the fatal mistake and one which Bremer refused to change when it was still possible to influence the outcome.

On de-Ba'athification, even the experts in Baghdad were not consulted. 'By nightfall, you'll have driven 30,000 to 50,000 Ba'athists underground,' the CIA station chief in Baghdad warned Bremer.[93] In the words of one old Iraqi soldier, 'They're all insurgents now. Bremer lost his chance.' In the same interview, Hoon said that he had argued with Rumsfeld against the summary dismissal of Iraq's 350,000-strong army and police forces 'but I recognised that it was one of those judgement calls. I would have called it the other way.' Blair had no 'direct input'. One official said 'his mind was elsewhere', another that he no longer had 'any more of a personal interest in stabilising Iraq'. Blair told Mandelson 'That's chiefly America's responsibility, not ours'.[94] According to Colonel Lawrence Wilkerson, Powell's former chief of staff, in dealing with Iraq Bush was 'too aloof, too distant from the details of postwar planning. Underlings exploited Bush's detachment.'[95] But Bush was never a pawn; he made the big moves, but sometimes without knowing all the positions on the chessboard. He took Powell's advice all too rarely, Rumsfeld's and Cheney's all too frequently, but he was still choosing for himself. Bush's problem was that he had created what Rice called in August 2003 'the dysfunctional US government'.[96] As the journalist Bob Woodward concluded, around Bush, 'the whole atmosphere too often resembled a royal court, with Cheney and Rice in attendance, some upbeat stories, exaggerated good news, and a good time had by all'.[97] The reality was that it wasn't just Bush's government that was dysfunctional, it was Bush himself as Commander in Chief.

One of the ironies of the dysfunction of Bush's administration is that the Cabinet committee structure still worked, but only in some areas – usually those where Rumsfeld did not hold departmental responsibility. Rumsfeld could normally only be reined in by the National Security Council or ad hoc meetings of the principals called by Rice to resolve disputes. One area where inter-departmental cooperation worked well on Iraq was over money. Here the US Treasury played the lead role, initially under Treasury Secretary O'Neill and his under-secretary, John Taylor, who stayed until 2005.[98] Obtaining money from Saddam Hussein's accounts in American banks, totalling $1.7 billion, Bush authorised 237.5 tons of US banknotes from $1 to $20 to be sent to Iraq on 20 March 2003. They were made available to pay Iraqis in the early days, helping to lift morale. The money was delivered by a fleet of Boeing 747s and distributed by armed convoys to 240 sites in Iraq – no mean feat. It was exchanged for old dinars, which were then dyed, taken away in trucks and incinerated. The new dinar introduced in October 2003 was popular. In late 2006 General David Petraeus reported on how in the early days US dollars found in Saddam's palaces, amounting to $1 billion, were imaginatively used by the US military to finance building schools and hospitals and repairing roads and bridges, separate from the overall reconstruction effort, which was less successful. By 2004, Iraq oil exports were being paid for in US dollars, and this helped finance the Iraqi government. The Army 336th Finance Command and US Treasury offices together in April 2003 established a reliable system and a working finance ministry and central bank. So not everything in Iraq failed; in some areas pre-planning worked and Cabinet members worked together. If only the same relationships could have been enforced by Bush between the Pentagon and State Department with regard to security planning in the aftermath, the core issue on which his dysfunctional government failed.

The figure Bush seems to have trusted most and worked directly with was General Tommy Franks, the regional commander for Afghanistan and Iraq, 'a tall, hot-tempered Texan' who openly disparaged the Joint Chiefs of Staff.[99] In his book *Fiasco*, Thomas Ricks, the former *Wall Street Journal* senior Pentagon correspondent and later in the same role at the *Washington Post*, describes Franks 'as a product of his Army and his faults reflected those of that institution. The Army went into Iraq with a considerable amount of hubris.'[100]

Bush imbibed that hubris. Speaking like a cocky sheriff in a cowboy movie, he had promised the American people after the fall of the Taleban government in Afghanistan that Osama bin Laden would be taken 'dead or alive'. He was derided for these words it was reported, by his wife mimicking his language and exaggerating his 'Wild West' tone. She was undoubtedly an influence in checking her husband's hubris, a role already described as undertaken in 1940 by Clementine Churchill.

In Iraq, when it became evident that Saddam had prepared for an organised resistance to a successful invasion and that insurgents were about to cause the occupying forces great difficulties, Bush's response was to say, 'Bring 'em on!' He seemed in the early period to give little thought to how to win more support from influential Sunnis, or how to get Iran to influence the Shi'ite majority. Ignoring the diplomatic initiative in May 2003 by Iran in terms of achieving success in Iraq was very shortsighted.

How much did Bush really know about the negotiations with Iran, which had started in 2002? In May 2003 a secret proposal was sent by Iran to the State Department for a 'grand bargain' with 'full transparency', aimed at assuring the USA that Iran would not develop nuclear weapons. The proposal also offered to end 'any material support to Palestinian opposition groups' and turn Hamas and Hezbollah into 'mere political organisations'. Did Bush abort the planned meeting in Geneva without knowing how seriously it had been pursued by his own government's senior officials?[101] Iran was at its weakest point in May with the USA apparently firmly entrenched militarily in Iraq. Yet there were enough signs of a developing insurgency to have made it the very best moment for the USA to cut a deal with the Iranians, sure in the knowledge that once Iraq was a stable democratic state it would be much easier to ensure Iran abandoned nuclear weapons and also followed down the democratic path.

This was the compelling logic for starting to develop a dialogue with Iran in 2002 before the invasion of Iraq. It is easy to forget that the Iranians had been helpful to the USA over the invasion of Afghanistan, in helping to mobilise the Northern Alliance, as well as throwing out al-Qaeda operatives from the holy city of Mashhad when they crossed over into Iran in 2002. Given that toppling Saddam was bound to bring the Shi'ite majority to power in Iraq, the potential for mischief-making from Iran was obvious. Yet Bush and Blair decided that they could deal with Shi'ites in Iraq while rejecting a wider Iranian dialogue. It is hard to be sure what lay behind Bush's decision, but overconfidence was certainly a factor. His refusal to have any dialogue with Syria was also damaging for they could have influenced the Sunnis in Iraq. The Sunni–Shi'ite relationships were bound to be fraught, with a Sunni minority in any evolving democratic system, having to get used to no longer being the dominating power. Going alone in 2003 Bush and Blair laid their forces open to insurgents supported and sustained across borders with Syria and Iran, which they never sought to close. The Iraq Inquiry needs to know what was Blair's direct input to Bush about the proposal from Iran to negotiate. The year 2003 was the time for preventive action. It was not wise for Blair in 2011 to blame Iran for all his and Bush's failings in Iraq. Nor after his own failures in Iraq and Afghanistan was he credible in campaigning for the bombing of Iranian nuclear installations. A period of serious reconsideration by Blair of where he went wrong would have been a better course of action before he began to hint at another military intervention in evidence to the Iraq Inquiry.

Bush, who started with focused meetings and confidence in the military and the CIA, revealingly, later began to blame them. He said 'Tommy Franks and the generals' had looked him in the eye and had assured him that the Iraq invasion was undertaken with 'the right plan with the right troop levels'. Franks probably believed this when he said it, before his retirement, but even when he said it, it was disputed within the Pentagon among senior military figures. By the summer of 2003 it was patently not true. Bush also claimed that the head of the CIA, George Tenet, had been extremely bullish, recalling his claim over WMD in Iraq: 'It's a slam dunk case,' a basketball term meaning certain success.[102] Yet Tenet in his account, published in 2007, claims he 'told the President that strengthening the public presentation was a "slam dunk", a phrase that was later taken completely out of context' and had haunted him ever since it appeared in Woodward's book.[103] Tenet was attacked in a letter to his publisher by former CIA officials for ignoring the information from a high-level member of Saddam's inner circle that Iraq had no past or present contact with Osama bin Laden, and yet he went before Congress in February 2003 to testify that Iraq did have such links. Tenet had also sat behind Colin Powell when he briefed the world, in the Security Council meeting on 5 February 2003, on US intelligence about Iraq's WMD. The 'blame game' has become a feature of the Iraq fiasco. In a BBC radio interview Lawrence Wilkerson said that he wished he had resigned in 2004 over Guantanamo. He added that he was reading Tenet's book and hearing Tenet give interviews and thinking some people in the CIA had 'lied' to Powell before his Security Council meeting on 5 February 2003.[104]

In his memoirs Bush cites his second error over the Iraq war "was the intelligence failure on Iraq's WMD. Almost a decade later, it is hard to describe how widespread an assumption it was that Saddam had WMD. Supporters of the war believed it; some opponents of the war believed it; even members of Saddam's own regime believed it. We all knew that intelligence is never one hundred per cent certain; that's the nature of the business. But I believed that the intelligence on Iraq's WMD was solid. If Saddam didn't have WMD, why wouldn't he just prove it to the inspectors? Every psychological profile I had read told me Saddam was a survivor. If he cared so much about staying in power, why would he gamble his regime by pretending to have WMD? Part of the explanation came after Saddam's capture, when he was debriefed by the FBI. He told agents that he was more worried about looking weak to Iran than being removed by the coalition. He never thought the United States would follow through on promises to disarm him by force."[105]

On 24 September 2003 Bush had a private dinner with Paul Bremer and their wives in Washington. On seeing Bremer's organisation chart showing twenty people reporting to him, Bush said, 'Look, I know you went to business school but I went to business school. You've got too many direct reports.'[106] On 27 October, Bush again saw Bremer, this time with Condoleezza Rice, Donald Rumsfeld and Richard Myers, the chairman of the Joint Chiefs of Staff, in the room. But later, working out with Bremer in the White House gym, Bush asked about Rumsfeld, 'Does he really micromanage?' and seemed surprised when Bremer said he did. Bush must have been one of the few people in Washington not to know this was Rumsfeld's besetting sin. Another little sign that the Commander-in-Chief had no real grip on his administration.

Politically the time for Bush to reconsider his inability to control the insurgency and review his absurdly optimistic predictions was on 12 November 2004, ten days after he had won re-election as President. The second attempt to deal with Fallujah was still underway when Powell saw both Bush and Blair at the White House. Powell said, 'We don't have enough troops . . . We don't control the terrain.'[107] This was also, by then, the view of Bremer. The following month Bush was being cabled by the CIA station chief in Baghdad, 'We face a vicious insurgency, we are going to have 2,000 dead.' A few days later, on 17 December, a US military intelligence expert told Bush to his face about the insurgency, 'It's robust, it's well fed, it's diverse. Absent some form of reconciliation it's going to go on and that risks civil war. They have the means to fight this for a long time.'[108] Bush needed to recognise that he had to change course and decide to deploy more troops. It was only after electoral defeat in the mid-term elections in 2006 that Bush did agree to send a 'surge' of 21,000 extra troops to Baghdad. Many military commentators thought that by now this was too late and still involved an insufficient number.

But the 'surge' did have a beneficial effect. It may be that part of Bush's change of mind was being driven by dire events, but also by the quiet influence of his father, his wife and Condoleezza Rice. Hubris syndrome is acquired and associated with the exercise of power and therefore potentially it can fade when power diminishes. This is what appears to have happened in Bush's case. Ignited by 9/11, his hubris peaked in 2003 when boasting of 'Mission Accomplished'. It declined after 2006 and seemed virtually to have gone in retirement by 2011. Then Bush and President Obama jointly attended the 10th anniversary of 9/11 at Ground Zero in a healing and dignified way. This more modest Bush won the admiration of former critics including myself.

In relation to the law, from the early stages of the war Bush's approach mirrored that of his Attorney General, Alberto Gonzales. Namely that the al-Qaeda threat rendered 'obsolete Geneva's strict limitations on [the] questioning of enemy prisoners'.[109] He sought to avoid the constraints of international law on interrogation and detention after military intervention. Bush believed 'the war on terrorism ushered in a new paradigm', that the Geneva Conventions did not apply to al-Qaeda and that the Taleban prisoners were 'unlawful combatants' who had lost their PoW status.[110] These decisions were heavily criticised.[111] Bush, a lawyer, acted unilaterally with little or no consultation with friends or allies. For example he issued the order for a military commission to indict and try detainees without consulting his National Security Adviser and Condoleezza Rice told him that if it occurred again she or Gonzales would be forced to resign. In effect Bush ripped up long-standing inter-national agreements and announced that America would do as it liked. The resulting damage worldwide to American credibility was highlighted by the treatment of prisoners taken in Afghanistan, prisoners held in Guantanamo, and later by what happened in Iraq's Abu Ghraib jail when US personnel taunted and abused Muslim prisoners. Something similar was done by UK soldiers.

The 2011 Report by Sir William Cage on British army brutality and the killing of Iraqi civilians documents a substantial cover-up. The Report reflects very badly on the Ministry of Defence courts martial. As to the Blair Government's involvement there will be renewed questioning on whether successive Defence Ministers gravely misled the Joint Parliamentary Committee on Human Rights concerning the treatment of Baha Mousa. If they do so find, then Parliament must take the toughest sanctions to the point of insisting on resignations of MPs.

International opinion began to object to the policy of secret 'rendition' of terrorist suspects to countries whose regimes were prepared to adopt none-too-scrupulous methods of interrogation. Bush's claim that America condemned all torture seemed to many itself a contemptuous denial of obvious facts. Fortunately after a period the US legal system, when formally appealed to with regard to Guantanamo policy and in other areas, began to show from 2006 a readiness to challenge Bush's assumption of wartime presidential authority over Congressional law and the constitution. An important debate was opened up inside the USA on presidential war powers and continues under President Obama to this day.

Vice-President Dick Cheney in his memoirs gives both sides of the argument with selective quotes from President Obama's and his own speech on 21 May 2009. Obama who has not yet been able to close Guantanamo reaffirmed his pledge to follow "the imperative" of closing Guantanamo within a year, adding that the facility had "likely created more terrorists around the world than it ever detained." Indeed, he said, "By any measure, the costs of keeping it open far exceed the complications involved in closing it." On the matter of enhanced interrogation, he said, "I categorically reject the assertion that these are the most effective means of interrogation." He called the techniques Bush had authorised "torture". Such methods, he explained, had all arisen from the "expedience" of the previous administration, at an unacceptable cost to conscience and to the fundamental values of our country: "They are not who we are, and they are not America."

Cheney recalled the days after 9/11 and the absolute determination of the Bush administration to make sure the nation never again faced such a day of horror. "The key to ensuring that was intelligence, and we gave our intelligence officers the tools and lawful authority they needed to gain information, some of it known only to the worst of the terrorists, through tough interrogation, if need be. The interrogations had the sole purpose of gaining specific information that would save American lives and did in fact yield such information. I called again for the release of the memos that would prove just that."

To describe what the Bush administration had done as a program of torture, Cheney said, "is to libel the dedicated professionals who have saved American lives and to cast terrorists and murderers as innocent victims." Cheney also challenged the whole assumption that American values were abandoned, or even compromised, in the fight against terrorism:

'For all that we've lost in this conflict, the United States has never lost its moral bearings. And when the moral reckoning turns to the men known as high-value terrorists, I can assure you they were neither innocent nor victims. As for those who asked them questions and got answers: they did the right thing, they made our country safer, and a lot of Americans are alive today because of them.'[112]

I listened to the former director of MI5, Eliza Manningham-Buller, in the second of her Reith Lectures[113] on 13 September 2011 with a combination of fascination and admiration; a reminder of how valuable the BBC still is in twentyfirst century Britain. In answer to a question she said this:

"It's not the case that torture always produces false informa - tion, and that actually it's clear that torture *can* contribute to saving lives. But I don't think that's the point. I think the point is that it's not something that is right, legal or moral to do."

Edward Stourton, who was questioning her called this a fascinating position, because most people who don't like torture say it doesn't work. She was saying it does work, but it still shouldn't be done.

Listening I wondered how, if I was still Foreign Secretary, and in charge of MI6, I would act if I was asked to authorise torture involving a person who it was believed knew where a nuclear device about to be detonated, was hidden in central London? I am pretty sure I would do the following. I would authorise the torture and I would inform the Prime Minister that I had done so, not asking for approval but saying that I had instructed the Permanent Under-Secretary at the Foreign Office to report my decision to the Director of Public Prosecutions as soon as it was safe to do so, whether or not I was still Foreign Secretary. In this way, I hope one could balance conflicting imperatives, to do everything possible to protect the lives of the citizens of this country but also not to shirk from the fact that torture is against the law and that no-one, and certainly not a Foreign Secretary, could or should be above the due process of the law. It would be then for the Director of Public Prosecutions to decide if the case should be tried and for a jury to deliver a verdict.

Blair's hubris after the invasion

In Tony Blair's case, the reality of the invasion's aftermath, and the absence of post-conflict planning, in which he had taken so little serious interest beforehand, was made clear to him on 11 May 2003, only ten days after George W. Bush's 'Mission Accomplished' public relations exercise. John Sawers, the British Ambassador to Egypt, who had previously worked for Blair in No. 10 had been specially sent into Iraq by Blair. He wrote a memo entitled 'Iraq: What's Going Wrong'. His summary of the Americans' aftermath team under General Jay Garner was succinct: 'No leadership, no strategy, no coordination, no structure and inaccessible to ordinary Iraqis.' Sawers' clear view was that more troops were needed and he suggested that 'an operational UK presence in Baghdad is worth considering, despite the obvious political problem . . . one battalion with a mandate to deploy into the streets could still make an impact.' Sawers' view about the need for more troops was backed up by Major General Albert Whitley, the most senior British officer with the US land forces, serving in the US headquarters of Lieutenant General David McKiernan. The issue was whether to bring the British 16 Air Assault Brigade, in Iraq but due to return home, to Baghdad. The Sawers memo could hardly have been a more serious communication to a Prime Minister with thousands of troops at risk in Basra, for what affected Baghdad was soon bound to affect Basra too. But what then happened in Downing Street to the Sawers memo? We know it was also copied to the Foreign Secretary's private secretary, but did any Cabinet sub-committee meet to consider deploying more troops? What was the advice to the Secretary of State for Defence and through him to the Prime Minister? On 10 December 2009 Sawers, now Sir John, and head of MI6, gave evidence to the Iraq Inquiry[114] about his memo written to arrive on desks in London on 11 May 2003. He describes it as "my first significant report back to London, which I sent on the Sunday night, the day before Bremer arrived, [12 May] [stressing] that there were a number of big issues that needed to be addressed. I listed five." On the first issue he told the Inquiry that he thought it would be "a mistake to think that de-Ba'athification seriously contributed to the insurgency because I don't believe it did." He compared the Allies in 1945 excluding 2.5% of the German population from jobs because of their links to the Nazi party with what Bremer went on to propose which was only excluding 0.1% of the Iraqi population, ie 25 times fewer, proportionately, than was the case in Germany and even within that total Bremer was looking for scope to grant exemptions. He also said "the Iraqi army had disbanded itself, that the many conscripts had gone back home and the units had all dispersed. So the Iraqi army didn't exist, in many ways, except on paper when I arrived in early May." This evidence was very different from that given by the British Defence Secretary, Geoff Hoon, referred to earlier who believed the Iraq army had been disbanded by a US order and claimed he had argued with Rumsfeld "against the summary dismissal".

Sawers then went on:

"General Mike Jackson, who was then the newly appointed Chief of General Staff visited Baghdad in my first few days there . . . in discussion it became clear that part of the problem was the posture of the US army. They were in their tanks in their Darth Vader kit, with wraparound sunglasses and helmets and flak jackets and everything else, and there was no real rapport between the US army and the ordinary citizens of the capital. Mike Jackson, and I have to say I have some sympathy with this, thought there was a case of bringing a larger contingent of 'Paras' not just the 20 or so in the platoon, but a battalion of 'Paras' up to work with the Americans to demonstrate a different way of deploying in urban areas, and this was all part of what we had learnt in other places, in Northern Ireland and so on."

"I reported this as one option back to London, after I discussed it with Mike, but it was clearly a military matter. There were differences of view between the Chiefs of Staff on this. I think the officials in No. 10 were quite attracted by the idea but in the end the military advice that came to the Prime Minister was against doing this."

"Unfortunately, in some ways, the idea had gained some traction with the Americans, both in Washington and in Baghdad, who were quite attracted to the idea as well. So in a sense we marched them up to the top of a hill and then we marched them back down by raising the idea and then turning it down, and when the Prime Minister visited Basra towards the end of May, at the end of this little saga, Bremer said to him how sorry he was that Britain had decided against making available a battalion of 'Paras' to go to Baghdad."

In Blair's memoirs, amazingly, given the crucial importance of Sawers' recommendations sent to him on 11 May, he makes no reference to its content or gives any explanation why he did not follow its recommendation. But he writes only about how on his return after his visit to Basra at the end of May, "I called the key Ministers together and gave a series of instructions to get our help to the US on a better footing. We had thought they would handle the centre of the country and we the south. I realized after that visit that unless they succeeded, we would fail.

I had sent John Sawers, my former key foreign policy adviser, to Baghdad. He came to the same conclusion: the American operation needed a drastic boost. I also sent a strong note to George and we then spoke by phone." [115]

Sawers, under oral questioning, to the Iraq Inquiry,[116] went into more detail about his attitude as to why the British should move troops into Baghdad and what was the problem with the American forces posture:

"they had not been able to transition from war fighting to peacekeeping, that they had a heavy armoured division in place, whereas the much lighter (US) 101 Airborne Division up in Mosul were much lighter on their feet, much more engaged with the local population. The then unknown Major General David Petraeus was in charge and he showed what could be done in a city like Mosul, which was as divided and difficult to manage as Baghdad, but the 3 Infantry Division was not doing the task in what I thought was the best way. So it was partly style and that was my main concern."

"Bremer saw this as a serious problem as well, which was why he welcomed the idea of a parachute battalion from the UK coming up to the capital. He was also concerned about overall troop numbers and he raised this with President Bush on a number of occasions because the US plan was for a rapid drawdown of forces. Indeed the British plan was also for a rapid drawdown of forces. I do not have the exact numbers but I think the Americans were aiming by the summer to be down to 60 per cent of their force levels at the height of the conflict and the British forces were planning to be down to 40 per cent of their maximum forces. So both Washington and London were planning for very far-reaching reductions in force levels."

"It seemed to me, partly because the Iraqi regime had never been properly defeated and that the insurgency was growing, that the *après guerre*, the period after the war, was going to be more demanding than the war itself and that this needed to be taken fully into account. Bremer was very much of that mind and he raised it a number of times with Secretary Rumsfeld and, I believe, with President Bush and achieved a slowing down of the US force levels."

We know that Sawers returned to London a week after he had met Bremer and attended a regular weekly meeting of the Chiefs of Staff where "the main issue on the Chiefs of Staffs' minds was whether we should send a battalion of the Parachute Regiment up to Baghdad to support the US efforts to maintain control of the capital." At this moment Blair should have intervened, that is if he had a view. The Chiefs could and in my view, should have been left under no illusion that the Prime Minister believed this was a decision with a huge political content. He should not have left the issue for Sawers to argue through. He, as a diplomat, had with both bravery and foresight gone further than he could reasonably be expected to do. Nor could General Jackson, recently beaten by Walker for the position of Chief of Staff, go much further. At this point a Prime Ministerial intervention was a *duty;* one way or the other the Chiefs were entitled to know his view. It remains to be seen when the Inquiry reports but from the evidence to the Inquiry it is not clear that Blair had a view. This episode is one on which the Inquiry cannot avoid taking a view.

On 1 February 2010 Lord Walker of Aldringham, who had become the Chief of Defence Staff on 1 May following on from Admiral Boyce, gave evidence to the Iraq Inquiry. He admitted to the Inquiry that he was aware of Shinseki's concerns and Rumsfeld's wish to take Iraq with quite a small force would leave a gap and that not enough troops had been sent to Iraq and he also mentioned that he would have preferred the British to be in the northern part of Iraq had it been possible to come in from Turkey. He had himself visited Baghdad very early in May 2003 before the situation had deteriorated. The following exchange then took place in the Inquiry. [117]

Sir Lawrence Freedman: There were approaches made by the United States to send 16 Air Assault to Baghdad and I think you had opposed that. Is that correct?

General Lord Walker: Yes

Sir Lawrence Freedman: Why was that?

General Lord Walker: You say I opposed it. We, the Chiefs, collectively, opposed it. Well, I say "collectively", we didn't all agree about it, but it seemed to me that this was in the early days and I think it must have been shortly after John Sawers' arrival, which would have been mid-2003. We had enough of a problem keeping our logistic supplies and the expertise needed down in the south. I also came to the conclusion, having seen Baghdad, this vast, sprawling city in which there weren't enough troops really to control it in the true sense of the word – I think the Americans must have had about 130,000 at one stage, of which about 80 [presumably meaning 80,000] were in Baghdad and we were offering to send up to 3,000 or 3,500. I did not think they were going to alter the price of fish, to be honest.

But at that time we thought we were quite good and I think there was a view that, if we could get some nice smiling 'Paras' on the streets of Sadr City, this would transform Baghdad overnight, and I am afraid I didn't subscribe to that.

I have quoted extensively from this part of a mass of evidence taken during the Iraq Inquiry because I believe it reveals the nub of why the handling of the aftermath in Iraq was such a disaster. Both President Bush and Prime Minister Blair, despite contrary evidence stuck hubristically to the view that they could get away with far too few troops on the ground. The number proved totally insufficient to control the urban areas, the very situation they were warned about. In evidence to the Iraq Inquiry[118] Admiral Boyce was reminded about the Ministry of Defence briefing of the Prime Minster on 15 January 2003 where the record of the meeting has the Prime Minister being told:

> "Aftermath planning was still quite immature and any rapid regime collapse followed by a power vacuum could result in internecine fighting between the Shia and Sunni populations, particularly in Baghdad, and adventuring by adjacent countries and ethnic groups that irretrievably fractured the country."

One of the Committee, Sir Roderic Lyne, actually said to Boyce, "So you had got it pretty well right?"

In another exchange Boyce clearly reveals the fundamental divide in the American military.

Sir John Chilcot: I suppose what I am asking is you would have been aware of the fact that there were divided opinions even within the American military at senior level?

Admiral The Lord Boyce: Yes, I was aware of it and there were I guess two reasons why there were division of ideas. There was the one bunch of people probably, certainly, led by Rumsfeld who definitely had a view that we do war fighting, we don't do peacekeeping or nation building. That was not just an idle mantra. That was passionately, passionately believed, and combined with the new idea about warfare, where everything could be done electronically or by high tech and therefore didn't require boots on the ground, it meant you went in with lots and lots of high tech with as few people as possible, did what you needed to do and got out fast. So that sort of attitude of mind "We do war fighting and furthermore we do it at this very high tech level", meant you were going to have a very anorexic force level in terms of number of bodies, of soldiers. That was one view that was certainly held by Rumsfeld.

Then you have the other side, like the Chief of the Army, Shinseki, who believed that that was not a very sensible course of action, because he could see (a) the high tech didn't necessarily give you what you wanted, and also the need for having the troops on the ground when you got down to providing advice and security and a stabilization force until you got your new structures in place. I think more people sided with him than they did with Rumsfeld frankly but that's my personal feeling rather than – I can't give you any factual evidence on that.

There is no shadow of doubt that Tony Blair as Prime Minister was given a totally correct assessment of the risks ahead. Yet there is no acknowledgement of this in his memoirs. He summarises the position of what went wrong without any admission that he had been warned that this could happen or that there was any substance in the criticism that he was responsible. He writes:

"What happened in Iraq after May 2003 was, at first, relatively benign. There was looting and some violence; some attacks on coalition forces, but they were containable . . . What happened was that the security situation deteriorated. It did so in part as a result of Iraqi elements acting of their own accord, of tribal, religious and criminal groups deciding to abort the nascent democracy and to try to seize power. But the critical, extra dimension, the one which translated a difficult situation into near chaos, was the linking up of these internal dissident factions with al-Qaeda on the one hand and Iran on the other." [119]

The evidence available appears to suggests that Sawers' plea was in effect ignored by Blair and that he was content to accept the advice of the Chiefs of Staff. But he must have known that Jackson had been in Baghdad and had supported Sawers' memo. The truth is that there was a difference of opinion in the Chiefs of Staff between Jackson and Walker, not unreasonably the other two Chiefs from the Air Force and the Navy sided with the Chief of Defence, General Walker. But it is in exactly this sort of situation – politial as well as military - that a Prime Minister is fully entitled and indeed ought to intervene with his own judgement. Judging by the history of Lloyd George, Churchill, Thatcher and John Major, their engagement and attention to detail during their wars, this was sadly lacking in the case of Blair's conduct. This is something I hope Sir Martin Gilbert, the Second World War historian on the Iraq Inquiry, will concentrate on. And not just on this most crucial occasion but on some others as well.

Blair's inattention was crucial and its origins are in the nature of hubristic incompetence. It has been argued by Sawers, in Blair's defence, that this was a purely military matter to be decided solely by the Chiefs. But this is 'diplomatic speak' to protect his political master. It is nonsense. Blair heard that the US, in the person of Bremer wanted British troops on the ground in Baghdad. He also must have known that there were influential people in Washington, who were keen for the UK to send forces up from Basra to Baghdad. Why was this?

It was because they knew that such a UK deployment would be bound to carry weight with President Bush and possibly make him challenge his Secretary of Defense, Rumsfeld. They knew that the whole issue of the number of US troops needed in Baghdad as well as their posture needed to go to the highest level and to be decided by the President. If the British Prime Minister directly decided to deploy troops in Baghdad then the President would become involved. I can find no evidence that there was any collective discussion amongst Ministers about this conflict of views within the Chiefs of Staff. Sawers, having been at their meeting, must have reported back to the Foreign Secretary and to the Prime Minister in some way. This is something that the Inquiry, to be credible, must find out about and pronounce on.

The vital significance of all this is that, in my judgement, had Blair responded with more troops, it would have been impossible for Bush to refuse to do so as well with the press reports of looting and chaos being seen as the reason for the British deployment. Donald Rumsfeld would not have then been allowed to 'offramp' the 16,000 soldiers of the 1st Cavalry Division. This was one of the rare moments to nip the insurgency in the bud. As Prime Minister, Blair should have acted. Instead an opportunity was lost and the insurgency in Iraq dragged on for many more years.

Jeremy Greenstock, formerly Britain's Ambassador to the UN, who was sent from New York to Baghdad to follow Sawers, later said of the days following victory:

"No-one, it seems to me, was instructed to put the security of Iraq first, to put law and order on the streets first. There was no police force, no constituted army except the victorious invaders and there was no American general, who I could establish, who was given the accountable responsibility to make sure that the first duty of any government – and we were the government – was to keep law and order on the streets. There was a vacuum from the beginning in which looters, saboteurs, the criminals, the insurgents, moved very quickly."[120]

On 29 August 2003 another turning point in Iraq came with the attack on the Imam Ali mosque in Najaf, which killed Ayatollah Baqir al-Hakim, an influential moderate Shi'ite religious leader.

Blair's generalised hubris had begun to desert him by the end of the year. We now know that from Easter 2003 he was under considerable stress, but it was from a matter unrelated to Iraq or his duties as Prime Minister, and over which the press collectively showed great restraint, not reporting on what they rightly considered to be a genuinely private, family matter. When the Prime Minister looked tired and strained through 2003 and 2004, those people in and around Whitehall who knew put it down to this additional stress. But his self-confidence about Iraq appeared shaken too. At the annual diplomatic reception at Buckingham Palace, on 4 November 2003, I had another interesting, but shorter, talk with Blair about Iraq. He insisted on us sitting down together for a serious discussion in the ballroom and ignoring for a time the foreign diplomats circulating around. This was a very different Tony Blair from the messianic leader I had talked to over dinner in July 2002. He was far less sure of himself and he appeared somewhat chastened by events: the inability to find any WMD in Iraq was clearly troubling him. I felt rather sorry for him and tried to cheer him up. But I was, by then, fearful of a debacle, annoyed at his incompetence and felt he had twisted the intelligence.

It was also becoming clearer as every month passed that No. 10 was not going to get its "Baghdad bounce" in the opinion polls on the back of which Blair could call a euro referendum. So the other great 'Caesarist' project to which Blair was dedicated, fortunately looked like collapsing. But this did not stop Blair making concession after concession to the integrationists in the negotiations on Giscard d'Estaing's draft Constitutional Treaty. This continued after the Treaty was rejected by the Dutch and the French in their referendums and over its successor the Treaty of Lisbon, on which there was no pledged referendum.

By January 2004 I had become convinced that Blair had permanently lost authority and credibility and should choose an early moment to step down and take another job. I wrote an article in the *Sunday Times* on 4 January entitled 'Self-rule by Blair gives him a Suez crisis'. While still believing that toppling Saddam Hussein was a legitimate policy I suggested that Blair should step down as Prime Minister no later than the expected 2005 general election. I wrote:

> Blair's authority has been severely, probably irreparably, damaged over Iraq, not just in his party but within the country . . . A well-conducted exit would make it more likely that Blair's Prime Ministership would be well regarded by history. There are other opportunities that lie ahead for Blair, not least perhaps as the next head of the World Bank.

Though subsequently Paul Wolfowitz was appointed to head the World Bank, the USA has for some time been interested in the chairmanship of the International Monetary Fund and letting a European run the World Bank. Blair never again recovered the authority and trust of the British people and

Parliament that any Prime Minister requires when soldiers are being killed in battle.

We now know Blair had actually decided to step down as Prime Minister around late May/early June 2004. Whether he had simply recognised it was time to leave, was depressed or was very stressed, or as is more likely a combination of all three, remains unclear. For the country it was the right time for him to go, but he was dissuaded from resigning by some of his loyal friends in the Cabinet. It had some parallels with President Johnson's wish to resign when depressed in 1965 after an operation and when things were going wrong in Vietnam. [121]

The Chancellor of the Exchequer, Gordon Brown, not unreasonably wanted Blair to step down so that he could succeed him, but he apparently helped dissuade Blair, thinking that it would be better for Blair and for the Labour Party if the Prime Minister stepped down in the autumn, around the time of the annual Labour Party conference. Blair's heart problems, which started in October 2003 and are discussed later in this book, may have returned at the time of his visit that summer with Cherie to the Sardinian home of the Italian Prime Minister, Silvio Berlusconi, but this was never substantiated. A family friend of the Blairs, Lord (Melvyn) Bragg, the writer and host of *The South Bank Show*, admitted in public later that Blair had been under tremendous stress that summer, saying in September 2004, 'In my view the real stress was personal and family, which matters most to him.'[122]

On 14 July 2004 the so-called Butler report, on failures of

intelligence prior to the invasion, was published.[123] When a former Cabinet Secretary such as Lord Butler is asked to conduct an inquiry on the committee of which the Prime Minister places a former Cabinet colleague, the Prime Minister knows that any criticism will need to be deftly drafted so as to reflect a consensus and thereby fall well short of calls to resign. But new facts on Blair's handling of intelligence have emerged from the Iraq Inquiry and are discussed in the Conclusion.

By the time the Labour Party conference came around, however, Blair had told his Cabinet colleagues that not only had he changed his mind about stepping down but that he was staying on to lead them into the next election. This he made public on 30 September 2004. But he went on to say that that election would be his last. This was not a well-thought-through statement, but one announced to damp down public speculation about his health, knowing that next day he would have to go into hospital. He was admitted as an outpatient for a catheter ablation, a treatment for an irregular heartbeat.

Misleading intelligence

Colin Powell, in his ill-advised statement to the UN on 5 February 2003, using intercepts about Republican Guard Corps commanders discussing removing the words 'nerve agents', mistakenly took this, because of prior Iraqi deceit, as yet more evidence of Iraqi bad faith. Since then it has been confirmed the words were actually part of an Iraqi attempt to ensure compliance with UN resolutions.[124] Powell, to his credit, has since apologised for his mistaken presentation to the UN. Yet he was correct to say then that 'Saddam Hussein has investigated dozens of biological agents causing diseases such as gas gangrene, plague, typhus, tetanus, cholera, camel pox, and haemorrhagic fever and he also has the wherewithal to develop smallpox'. In Tyler Drumheller's book *On the Brink*, the former head of CIA operations in Europe calls into question, more than the Butler report does, MI6's and his own government's reliance on a secret Iraqi agent for the Germans. German intelligence was relaying information to the CIA from an Iraqi chemical engineer codenamed Curveball, referred to in the Introduction.

Curveball alleged that Iraq had a biological weapons programme located in mobile laboratories and this claim was used in Powell's UN speech. According to George Tenet however in a detailed rebuttal this was done in good faith and he was never warned by Drumheller, or anybody else, before Powell's speech about reports of German or CIA doubts about Curveball.[125] German intelligence, however, told MI6 and the CIA that Curveball was an alcoholic and a fabricator and his allegations should not be accepted.[126] In the US the bipartisan Silberman – Robb Commission after the war investigated the Curveball matter. They found that Curveball, though a brother of one of the aides to Ahmed Chalabi, the leading figure in the Iraqi National Congress, he was not an INC source. Also that the INC had not significantly influenced the US prewar intelligence over Iraq.

The Butler report, unusually, also went beyond its remit into intelligence failings before the war and commented, albeit in Whitehall language made famous in *Yes, Minister*,[127] on the nature of Blair's decision-making process, singling out for criticism his personalised sofa-style way of making key decisions: 'We are concerned that the informality and circumscribed character of the government's procedures . . . risks reducing the scope for informed collective political judgement.'

In the run-up to the 2005 general election, Blair tried initially to campaign on his own, downplaying the electoral role and importance of Gordon Brown. This strategy failed in terms of public opinion, particularly with Labour Party supporters, and Brown was quickly brought back with a central role in the campaign, which Labour won, though with a greatly reduced majority and with only 35.2 per cent of the vote.[128] Yet Labour remained in power with only 9.6 million votes, down from 10.7 million in 2001 and 13.5 million in 1997.

Much to my surprise, two days before polling day, I received a telephone message from someone in the Cabinet close to Blair. Next day, on Wednesday 4 May, visiting the Temple of Apollo in the Peloponnese, where the concept of hubris has deep roots, I returned the call on my mobile. They were apparently worried about the rising Liberal Democrat vote and thought perhaps my endorsing Labour might check this. I declined to do so. I did not want a Conservative government, but I wanted the Liberal Democrats to do sufficiently well to ensure a greatly reduced Labour majority. I also hoped that such a result might convince

Blair to step down as Prime Minister thereafter, if need be by invoking his health for the political purpose of explaining his departure so soon after the general election. I discovered later on the very same day, on the eve of polling, when it had been proposed that I should declare for Labour, a tawdry interview had appeared in the *Sun* newspaper with Blair boasting about his sexual prowess.[129] Increased sexual drive is associated with manic behaviour but in this case the interview had every appearance of being carefully staged and timed to come out on the last day of the campaign, with no scope for a critical backlash. Blair's conduct in his high office was now well below an acceptable standard.

On winning the election, despite a massive reduction in the number of votes and seats, Blair's self-confidence returned. Claiming the country should now 'move on' over Iraq, his hubris syndrome revived though never becoming as marked as in 2001–3. His obsession about his legacy dominated decisions over the date of his promised resignation. He conveyed the impression that he and he alone could put into effect the programme of change his government had embarked upon for education, health and many other issues. Blair's tendency to rely only on his own judgement was not restricted to Iraq. In the years after the 2001 election No. 10 officials noted that it became commonplace for Blair to announce what his decisions were early on or right at the start of a meeting, not at the end. Blair's first Cabinet Secretary Robin Butler articulated the general problem in December 2004:

There is too much emphasis on selling, there is too much central control and there is too little of what I would describe as reasoned debate in government at all levels . . . The Cabinet now – and I don't think there is any secret about this – doesn't make decisions . . . All this is part of what is bad government in this country.[130]

In 2011 in a BBC 2 programme,[131] Butler said "It clearly came as a new idea that big decisions of government should be collective decisions of the Cabinet and he [Blair] never really during my time acclimatised to that." The presenter, Michael Cockerell, in the same programme reported "Tony Blair did not believe that the Cabinet was the right body to take big decisions. He preferred to work informally with his trusted advisers on the sofa in his office."

An article in the *Financial Times* on 12 September 2006 described 'the seven habits of a highly ineffective Prime Minister', reckoned to be failure to lead a collegiate administration; failure to manage expectations and follow through on ideas; adoption of the 'heroic CEO' model; top-down autocratic style; failure to listen to constructive, well-intentioned criticism; addiction to arbitrary targets and performance measures; failure to manage a stable and orderly succession. All are habits which have echoes in hubris syndrome.

No British Prime Minister since 1914, not Lloyd George, Churchill, not even Eden, over Suez, nor Margaret Thatcher has made the strategic decisions over war so personally and without systematically involving senior colleagues as Blair did. There are important safeguards in the pre-circulation of papers with the views of military commanders and key diplomats in the field being made known to a War Cabinet and this smaller group of ministers reporting regularly to the full Cabinet. This was the way Margaret Thatcher conducted the Falklands War in 1982 and the way John Major took decisions over the Gulf War in 1991. It was not the way in which the Iraq War was conducted by Blair. The full Cabinet essentially acted as a rubber stamp on decisions which Blair and a small coterie of selected colleagues and advisers took in No. 10 on foreign and defence policy. What was even more unusual in Blair's period in office was that a somewhat similar procedure was operated by Gordon Brown as Chancellor, for his decisions on economic policy. This dual 'presidency' arrangement was meekly accepted by the whole British Cabinet. It meant they were comprehensively bypassed. Labour must never allow this to happen again and must remember that it never happened under Attlee, Wilson or Callaghan.

Over Kosovo, President Clinton had been a restraining influence on Blair. Over Afghanistan and Iraq, Bush and Blair, working within a very small and closed group of advisers, seemed to ignite each other. Blair's capacity to delude himself and confidently believe that all would turn out right has often been commented on in other areas of his government's decision-making. This characteristic is compounded by his barrister's training to absorb his brief quickly and speak confidently on its contents. Too often, however, his knowledge on policy and on its execution, whether national or international, was superficial and lacked for detail when probed. This was his downfall regarding Iraq. One retired general, Sir Michael Rose, who was Adjutant General of the British army and commander of the UN protection force in Bosnia, went so far as to call for the Prime Minister to be impeached over Iraq because of 'a blunder of enormous strategic significance'.[132] Other senior generals talked more guardedly in public but trenchantly in private.

While still available to the US Congress, impeachment is no longer an option in the UK. Parliament used to be able to bring anyone to trial for 'high crimes and misdemeanours'. Warren Hastings was a famous case: in 1795, after a seven-year trial, the House of Lords gave a verdict of not guilty on all charges. An unsuccessful attempt was also made to impeach Lord Palmerston in 1848. The threat of impeachment is an important check on the power of a US President, as shown in the case of Richard Nixon. Its controversial invocation for Clinton's per-jury over his sexual conduct was, in my view, correct but so was Congress right to refuse to actually impeach him. Nevertheless for his false responses in his deposition, Clinton was given a two year suspension of his law licence in Arkansas and a $25,000 fine.[133] The very potential power of impeachment serves a useful purpose, reminding serving US Presidents that they are not above the law or challenge and that there is a higher authority than themselves which can even remove them from power in between elections. In the UK that power lies with a parliamentary vote or the overt withholding of support by the MPs of the Prime Minister's own party or as in the case of Lloyd George by his larger coalition partner, the Conservatives. The Dardanelles Commission in 1916 examined in some detail the machinery of government as well as the reasons for that military calamity in February 1915. The commission made two reports in 1917 and 1918, much of which was initially kept private so as not to jeopardise future operations. According to one historian the commission came to the conclusion that 'the operation had been ill-conceived and ineptly executed, with the vain expenditure of thousands of valuable lives'.[134] Winston Churchill as First Lord of the Admiralty was judged in part responsible for the Dardanelles defeat and was demoted to Chancellor of the Duchy of Lancaster at the end of May 1915. He later resigned to join the army and fight in France. The growing realisation of the incompetence of the government's early handling of the war meant that in December 1916 Herbert Asquith stepped down as Prime Minister to be replaced by David Lloyd George. Interestingly, the commission examined the machinery of government, the working of the Imperial Defence Committee, the War Council and the responsibilities of professional military advisers. It examined whether senior military commanders were answerable just to their own minister or whether their responsibility extended more widely, to the collective meetings with other ministers. It also considered how to resolve the issues when there was a conflict between the military and the politicians. I argued for something like the

Dardanelles Commission in a debate in the House of Lords on 29 June 2006.[135] Whether the Iraq Inquiry established in 2009 will have a lasting impact depends on the courage of its members. It was a great mistake that after Anthony Eden's resignation as Prime Minister having in December 1956 lied about the clandestine arrangement with Israel for militarily intervening on the Suez Canal that no independent inquiry took place. This handling of the Suez invasion and the unease over Eden's relationship with the British Armed Services and the Diplomatic Service deserved a thorough independent enquiry. The UK never learnt enough about Suez and as a consequence we have witnessed many of the same mistakes in Blair's handling of the invasion of Iraq. The same also applies to Afghanistan. A former Chief of the Defence Staff, Lord Guthrie, in 2006 called the manner of the UK and NATO deployment in Afghanistan 'cuckoo'. We are unlikely to get it but we should have an inquiry into Afghanistan as well.

Harold Wilson, as Prime Minister in 1964-70 faced a choice on whether to contribute British forces to the Vietnam War. He chose not to, believing he would not have sufficient influence on the handling of that war in part because of the character of President Lyndon Johnson. The President had an all encom - passing driving personality. He was diagnosed much later as suffering from bipolar disorder. In December 1964 Johnson wanted Wilson to send the Black Watch, a Scottish regiment, to Vietnam. It was for primarily presentational purposes and he revealed that to be his underlying attitude by actually saying to

Wilson that even a few pipers would be better than nothing! Nevertheless, apart from measured criticism in a speech in the White House in February 1968, Wilson supported an American presence in Vietnam and knowingly risked the jibe that he was 'the tail-end Charlie in an American bomber'. In a recorded telephone call to a third party Johnson refers to 'that creep Wilson' and once harangued him on the telephone: 'We won't tell you how to run Malaysia, and you don't tell us how to run Vietnam.' On another occasion Johnson threatened to withdraw financial support for the pound if Wilson did not send troops but Wilson countered by arguing that if the British withdrew troops from Malaysia and Hong Kong the pound would not need supporting.[136] Few politicians or historians, on either side of the Atlantic, have doubted that Britain was right to stay out of the Vietnam War and Wilson is already receiving more credit for his decision. It was open to Blair as late as February 2003, not to join in with the invasion of Iraq.

An example of the contempt, which often comes with hubris, that Blair developed and displayed to colleagues came from the account leaked from Downing Street of a conversation between him and Jack Straw after the result of the French referendum which rejected the EU constitution. Straw, no enthusiast for ever-increasing integration in Europe, had persuaded Blair, before the European Parliamentary elections in 2004 to promise a referendum, a change of position which was never discussed by the Cabinet. Straw had welcomed the French result. It was reported, after their conversation, that privately Blair turned to an aide and contemptuously remarked, 'Tart!' This remark, made within Blair's closed circle, was then deliberately given much publicity and, though formally denied, the story was never quashed.[137] Somewhat undiplomatically, Straw then described any military pre-emptive attack on Iranian nuclear installations as 'nuts'. This appeared quite deliberate, as if he feared Bush with Blair's support might use the existence of any announced threat, as part of a sensible negotiating stance over the Iran nuclear enrichment programme, to legitimise their acting pre-emptively. Straw was demoted by Blair in May 2006 and replaced by Margaret Beckett, someone with no experience of foreign affairs. Blair's Defence Secretary during the Iraq war, Geoff Hoon, remained loyal to the Prime Minister throughout, but was progressively demoted by him.

By the time of the Lebanon crisis in July–August 2006, with two new and inexperienced secretaries of state in the Foreign Office and the Ministry of Defence, there was no one to challenge Blair's refusal, along with Bush, to publicly endorse a ceasefire. It was an extraordinary omission. Even in Israel there was and, after the eventual ceasefire, continued to be detailed criticism of the nature of the Israeli air attacks on Hezbollah targets in Lebanon. They succeeded in destroying a large part of Lebanon's infrastructure but made little impact on Hezbollah's capacity to launch missile attacks. Bush and Blair were both party to the well-judged G8 summit communiqué from St Petersburg calling for a rapid deployment of a multilateral force. Had they both made an immediate contribution to the deployment of such a rapid reaction force to southern Lebanon it would have ensured an early ceasefire.

In a swaggering display at a press conference in Washington on 28 July, they both refused to put the weight of their diplomacy behind such a ceasefire. Almost alone among world leaders, they seemed to believe that repeated Israeli attacks from the air on targets in Lebanon, including houses and apartments in urban areas, would destroy Hezbollah. The informed criticism of Israeli strategy from inside Israel made their high-flown rhetoric about values appear totally cynical. Both the senior diplomats initially put in charge of Blair's secretariats disowned the policy, Sir Stephen Wall, who had retired, publicly and Sir David Manning, Ambassador in Washington, reportedly in private. Blair's stance was morally indefensible and also one that was doomed militarily. Blair then spoke in Los Angeles about an 'arc of extremism' now stretching across the Middle East', totally ignoring that it was his and Bush's failure to make a success of the Iraq invasion which had made by far the largest contribution to setting the region aflame and greatly strengthening Iran. Strangely, it was Lebanon, not Iraq, that triggered the moderate centre ground of Labour MPs at last to say that 'enough was enough'. They forced Blair to recognise that he had to say publicly in September 2006 that this would be his last party conference, something he had been resistant to doing.

Exactly how disastrous Iraq had become for Blair became clear when the medical journal the *Lancet* in October 2006 published a study from Johns Hopkins University estimating that 650,000 Iraqi civilians had died between March 2003 and July 2006. Typically, Blair's spokesman dismissed the study, saying, 'It was not one we believe to be anywhere near accurate.' Also Bush said, 'I don't consider it a credible report.' Yet inside the British government the Ministry of Defence's chief scientific adviser, as we now know, said the research was 'robust', close to 'best practice' and 'balanced'. He recommended 'caution in publicly criticising the study'. A Foreign Office official concluded that the government 'should not be rubbishing the *Lancet*'.[138] Blair now accepts 100,000 Iraqi casualties which is still far greater than any attributed so far to terrorism worldwide.

It was no surprise that public respect for Blair and Bush diminished to all-time lows when they contested the likely casualty figures. In my view, as a minimum, both leaders should have admitted casualty figures were far too high, they had made mistakes and regretted they had not applied different policies, but were trying nevertheless to help the new democratically chosen Iraqi government end the insurgency. I remain of the view that this human tragedy in Iraq could and should have been avoided and that, before the invasion, civil war was not an inevitability. The responsibility for these horrific events rests, in large part, on Bush and in no small part on Blair.

After the Republican Party lost control of the House of Representatives and the Senate in November 2006 Bush at last began to change his stubbornly held policies in Iraq. He sacked Donald Rumsfeld and appointed a sensible successor in Robert

Gates. Vice-President Cheney became less influential and Condoleezza Rice, as Secretary of State, talked Bush around to accepting dialogue with Syria and Iran in the context of regional conferences called by the elected Iraqi Prime Minister, Nouri al-Maliki. By April 2007 Bush, belatedly, was increasing US troop levels in Baghdad, while the UK was reducing its numbers around Basra. A new intelligent US military commander in Iraq, General David Petraeus, developed a different and better strategy for tackling the insurgency and stiffening the Iraqi army, much of it recommended in the Baker–Hamilton cross-party report. The USA was, at last, trying to win around the Sunni resistance movement, as distinct from the insurgents.[139]

Meanwhile for Blair, nemesis was approaching. The man who had won power in 1997 with a landslide majority of 179 seats was now being forced out of office by Labour MPs earlier than he wished, after bequeathing results so bad, in national elections in Scotland and Wales and local elections in England, that if repeated at a general election would have given the Conservatives a 54-seat majority. (*Sunday Times* on 6 May 2007.) Blair's self-indulgent long goodbye, in search of a legacy, damaged all around him. No British Prime Minister had started so well and yet ended so badly.

Gordon Brown

When Gordon Brown at last entered Number 10, he failed to do what John Major had done after succeeding Margaret Thatcher in 1990. Major convinced the British people that his was a totally fresh government and went on to win the general election in 1992.

On 20 June 2007 Gordon Brown, after ten years as Chancellor of the Exchequer and seven days from becoming Prime Minister, made remarks that were very revealing. He talked of 'the beginning of a new golden age for the City of London'. Having boasted for some time of ending 'boom and bust', in this speech he claimed that during the first decade of the twenty-first century, out of 'the greatest restructuring of the global economy, perhaps even greater than the Industrial Revolution, a new world order was created'. Within a few months of Brown's speech, banks were being nationalised or bailed out and the world was facing its worst economic crisis for more than seventy years. Soon over half of British banks were either nationalised or had the government as their largest shareholder.

Yet despite these hugely hubristic remarks, Brown did not have or develop hubris syndrome. Nor was hubris the biggest problem Brown faced as Prime Minister. There was too much inner tension brought out from self-doubt in his personality. He found it difficult to admit mistakes, not because he was super-confident but because there was an underlying lack of confidence. I sensed he knew when he had made mistakes and regretted them, but he believed as a tribal politician and a practitioner of the black arts of politics, mistakenly, that the admission of error was a demonstration of weakness, so any apology had to be dragged out of him. His bitten-down finger nails reflected anxiety depression and his mood swings, which made him difficult to work with, were compensated by real knowledge and a dedicated work ethic. A very complex and at times charming man, he was consumed by ambition to be Prime Minister and yet when he succeeded Tony Blair, his indecision stopped him from calling an early general election which he could have won.

To Brown's credit, he had always publicly recognised as Chancellor that joining the eurozone was a matter of timing and it was never in Britain's immediate interests to do so and that we needed to have a flexible exchange rate. The ability to depreciate by something between 25 per cent and 30 per cent since the 2008 crisis has been one of the advantages the UK still has within the EU. It means our economic crisis is more manageable than our fiscal crisis, which promises to remain dire for some years ahead. Brown's replacement as Chancellor, Alistair Darling, had the courage to warn in a deliberately frank interview early on that we were arguably facing the worst crisis in sixty years and then, when criticised by briefings from No. 10, compounded his offence by saying the worst in 100 years. Darling showed himself to be cool under fire. His and Brown's problem was that when the banks ran out of money for the second time they took on vast liabilities through the so-called Asset Protection Scheme. The UK from then on had to maintain international confidence in the manner and the timing of large public spending cutbacks and raised taxes so that it could fund its fiscal deficit, otherwise it risked its AAA credit rating and being forced to the IMF. This was the challenge the new coalition government of Conservatives and Liberal Democrats faced in 2010.

My contacts with Gordon Brown over the years had been minimal. But he did ask to see me on Wednesday 12 September 2007 in 10 Downing Street, the day before, with great publicity, he saw Margaret Thatcher. By Friday evening, while travelling between Chicago and Athens, I was being inundated with telephone calls from Sunday newspaper journalists who had been variously briefed by No. 10 that we had talked and that I was returning to the Labour Party. I had to correct this impression, which was untrue, while indicating that I wished Gordon Brown well personally.

In our long conversation it became pretty clear that Brown wanted me to advise him on the NHS, in effect as part of his GOAT – government of all the talents – initiative. For many good reasons it was not something that I was ready to undertake. Devoted though I am to the NHS, I doubted I would have had real influence, and I was out of date. Three years' virtual absence over Yugoslavia meant that my knowledge of the NHS was much less than it had been. Also Labour seemed to have moved too far from the internal market I had espoused in the 1980s to an external market in the NHS. In any case there was part of me that was disillusioned with Labour and wanted to remain independent. I had thought that New Labour might carry the flag for what the SDP would have been. But on that score Blair's record left me totally despairing. Furthermore, too many of my good friends had long been very critical of Gordon Brown and believed that he was not going to be a good Prime Minister. Strangely, I did not share their views and hoped he would return New Labour to social democracy. They said that I was too optimistic about his personality, his style of working and his readiness to return to Cabinet government, that he was too embroiled in the presidential model after having, in effect, operated a joint presidency, at the expense of the Cabinet, with Tony Blair. At times during the banking crisis the UK seemed to be benefiting from Brown's long Treasury experience and he gathered around him a good team for the G20 summit in London. He wisely used Mark Malloch Brown, an experienced UN diplomat who was a successful part of GOAT initiative, as was Ara Darzi, a distinguished surgeon, who added valuable expertise. The concept should be maintained. But sadly my friends' fears about Gordon Brown were shown to be more justified than my optimism.

What then are the key questions for assessing political leadership? Are we paying too high a price by overvaluing charismatic leadership and undervaluing other strengths? Allowing our Prime Ministers to behave as American Presidents is to forget the difference between the fusion of powers between the Prime Minister, Cabinet and Parliament and the separation of powers between the Presidents of the USA and Congress. It is noteworthy how high amongst postwar Prime Ministers is the standing of Clement Attlee. Decisive but not charismatic. Leader of a team of talented individuals, he set clear parameters but then, by and large, gave them their head. He was someone who felt no need to interfere in order to dominate and had little, if any, hubris in his make-up.

Susceptibility to hubris

In a book about Iraq entitled *Imperial Hubris*, Michael Scheuer, the former head of the CIA's Bin Laden Unit, claims, 'Arrogance is not the worst of it for America as she charges forward in the cause of instant democracy. That honor falls to the category of hubris, buttressed by ignorance.'[1] Even one of Tony Blair's most consistent supporters, the journalist Philip Stephens, wrote an article in the *Financial Times* on 14 July 2006 entitled 'Hubris is the thread running through Blair's many travails'. My own personal experience of Blair is that his hubris started to develop in 1999 during the Kosovo crisis and built up through the general election in 2001 until 9/11, when it developed fully. With George W. Bush there is a *prima facie* case that his hubris devel -oped only after 9/11. In running for office he appeared more modest in his foreign policy objectives and gave the impression of being more of an isolationist rather than an interventionist.

This leads to the question: why does hubris develop in some heads of government and not in others? I think the answer lies both in the particular external circumstances and in the internal personality of each individual. The cases of Bush and Blair illustrate both factors at work.

With regard to external factors, it has been suggested by the sociologist Daniel Bell that hubris is the condition of the age. 'Modern hubris is the refusal to accept limits, the insistence on continually reaching out. The modern world proposes a destiny that is always beyond: beyond morality, beyond tragedy, beyond culture.'[2] If this is the prevailing zeitgeist then it would be hard for a leader to resist it but I think Bell's generalisation may apply more to the United States than to Britain. It is certainly true that the beyond has always had a deep appeal to Americans, going back to the times when the frontier of the United States was being pushed ever westwards across the continent. Once America's territorial expansion had been completed the frontier became outer space, a new beyond to explore. And a powerful case can be made that this can-do mentality is something to celebrate rather than criticise and is central to American culture, especially its popular culture. The hero intent on ridding the world of evil and being ready to use whatever firepower may be necessary to do so is the staple of Hollywood films and of much American television. America's cult of youth also plays to this paradigm. Problems arise when this exuberance develops into hubris.

As an importer of American culture, Britain imbibes some of it but it is perhaps less pervasive a force than in the United States. Britain's culture is older, more European and its imperial ambitions are very much of the past. Perhaps a more specific factor liable to feed a tendency to the hubristic is the underlying belief in both countries that each has been and remains a force for good in the world. That this may in many respects be true is likely to strengthen its effect of providing a spur to a potentially hubristic leader to become a crusader in a wretched world. It is not without significance that both Bush and Blair are passionate Christians.

For the United States, the end of the Cold War undoubtedly created circumstances likely to encourage hubris in its leaders, for it emerged as the sole superpower. The absence of a counterforce to oppose it left the USA with the heady illusion that it was the 'indispensable nation' and the world was now its to control. This found expression in George W Bush's new National Security Strategy, launched in 2002, in which the United States reserved the right to take pre-emptive action where it thought fit and to deter 'potential adversaries from pursuing a military build-up in hopes of surpassing or equalling the power of the United States'. As his narrowly defeated rival in the 2000 presidential election, Al Gore, later put it:

President Bush now asserts that he will take pre-emptive action even if the threat we perceive is not imminent . . . An unspoken part of this new doctrine appears to be that we claim this right for ourselves – and only for ourselves . . . What this doctrine does is to destroy the goal of a world in which states consider themselves subject to the law, particularly in the matter of standards for the use of violence against each other. That concept would be replaced by the notion that there is no law but the discretion of the President of the United States.[3]

Britain's strategic position in the post-Cold War world is obviously far less powerful than America's and so less likely to encourage any latent hubris in its leaders. Nonetheless, its history has left Britain with a world role and a propensity to want to work closely with the United States which facilitates this. The phrase 'special relationship' has become too glibly used, fostering in Britain a self-deluding sense of importance vis-à-vis other nations. Yet because of the shared history and particularly shared language, the relationship which many American Presidents have had with British Prime Ministers is more intimate than that with most other heads of government. The effect is to make it likely that a British Prime Minister will feel caught up in the momentum of American foreign policy and in so far as that has a hubristic quality, it is likely to spread across the Atlantic. Policies towards Israel are where this relationship is most likely to exist.

As regards any personality traits which might incline a head of government towards hubris, several in Blair stand out very obviously. Firstly, as all his biographers make clear, his early passion was not politics but performing: both at school and at Oxford his interest was on the stage, performing as an actor or a member of a rock band. It appears that he was not led into politics by ideological conviction – he was, at school, a Conservative and he has always struggled to articulate a political philosophy that would root him in the Labour Party – but politics offered him a very large stage on which to perform. The brilliance and range of Blair's acting repertoire as a politician has been much noted. Politicians, particularly when they are not interested in detail, appear susceptible to narcissism but actor-politicians tend to be especially narcissistic – their political vision tends to have themselves at its centre, commanding the stage with all eyes upon them. Blair appears to like information on one or, at most, two pieces of paper; it is disputed how often he reads background material. It is hardly surprising that presentation and spin become so important for such politicians. But such narcissism in actor-politicians makes the hero role almost irresistible. The potential is, therefore, present for this to induce hubris.

A second trait of Blair's personality concerns his view of himself, in that he thinks he is always good. The journalist and author Geoffrey Wheatcroft has argued[4] that this is so strong in Blair that he is a latter-day antinomian – the name given to the sixteenth-century heretics who believed that 'to the pure all things are pure', meaning that whatever they did was, by definition, pure. Someone who believes he cannot act badly lacks the constraint on behaviour which the fear that he might would otherwise impose on him. Such people believe, particularly, that they cannot lie, so shading the truth can easily become a habit. Again, the link to hubris is obvious: to believe that you are always good removes an impediment to behaving hubristically. In 2003, Blair grandiosely boasted that he personally had 'got rid of four dictators in Kosovo, Sierra Leone, Afghanistan and Iraq'.[5] But in 1999 Kosovo was a NATO operation; only in Sierra Leone in 2000 did the UK keep control of its forces, which did establish security. Afghanistan in 2001 was initially a CIA operation, with Special Forces; in Iraq in 2003 there was a US-led military operation. The UK was the largest of the contributors but it was never remotely like the allied coalition that Bush's father put together to free Kuwait from its Iraqi invader in 1991 when John Major was P.M.

The nature of Blair's religious beliefs and the particular way he sees his relationship with God means that his Anglo-Catholic faith matters deeply to him. He tended to downplay it publicly as Prime Minister since in Britain a politician playing on their religion is definitely not an electoral asset, as it sometimes appears to be in the USA. However, in a television interview on 4 March 2006, and perhaps because he knew he was committed to stepping down as Prime Minister before another general election, Blair abandoned his reservations in talking about his religion and said, in relation to Iraq, 'If you have faith about these things then you realise that judgement is made by other people. If you believe in God, it's made by God as well.' The implication is that the accountability that really matters to Blair is not to the electorate but to God. If, however, he is already convinced of his own goodness, that accountability is not constraining as it would be to the believer aware of his own capacity to sin. The belief in God then becomes a spur to hubris rather than a constraint on it.

A further insight into Tony Blair's religious views comes, not surprisingly, from a totally unauthorised, and one of the best of his biographers, *The Blairs and Their Court*.[6] The authors, Francis Beckett and David Hencke rightly refused to be put off by Alastair Campbell's assertion "We don't do God". In truth, Tony Blair found "two things at Oxford: God and a guru. God was far and away the most significant discovery of his life. But Blair is the sort of Christian who is looking to religion for a complete answer to every ethical decision you may be called upon to make and for that you need more than God: you need a philosopher." Blair told the world in 1994, when he became leader of the Labour Party, who his philosopher was – "a guy called John Macmurray. It's all there." Dr Sarah Hale, a philosopher, made a comparative study of Macmurray and Blair's "Third Way" speeches.[7] She wrote that Blair's guru "had a pretty idiosyncratic take on Christianity which led him to refuse involvement with any church or denomination until he became a Quaker at the end of his life." She writes how Macmurray "set out in detail the kind of morality currently espoused by Blair, only to condemn it as false and evil."

Blair is now an openly declared Roman Catholic but while Prime Minister he was a closet Catholic attending Mass until told not to do so by Cardinal Hume. Blair could not resist even then when writing back to the Cardinal that he would desist, but adding, "I wonder what Jesus would have made of it."

Blair now spends some time in the US raising funds for his Faith Foundation. A former American episcopal priest, having

165

attended on behalf of a rich philanthropist a Blair fund raiser, asked me whether he should advise that a donation be made. Interestingly he said he had one anxiety; it appeared that Blair believed he could bring all the big religions of the world together but in his time as a priest in his experience, people like this soon went off and founded their own religion. Blair seems to have little regard for the wise warning of Reinhold Niebuhr in *Moral Man and Immoral Society*.[8] "The undoubted moral resources of religion seem to justify the religious moralists in their hope for the redemption of society through the increase of religio-moral resources. In their most unqualified form, these hopes are vain. There are constitutional limitations in the genius of religion which will always make it more fruitful in purifying individual life, and adding wholesomeness to the more intimate social relations, such as the family, than in the problems of the more complex and political relations of modern society."

In George Bush's case his born-again Christianity started with a meeting with the evangelist Billy Graham in 1986, in his family holiday home in Maine, while his father was Vice-President. He writes in *A Charge to Keep* how that sparked a change in his heart over the course of that weekend: 'Rev. Graham planted a mustard seed in my soul, a seed that grew over the next year. He led me to the path and I began walking. It was the beginning of a change in my life.' Bush sees his God not as a power to keep him in check but as the force that spurs him on. Not surprisingly, a playwright chose to highlight Bush's views as they might have been before he became President: 'I feel like

God wants me to run for President. I can't explain it, but I sense my country is going to need me. Something is going to happen and at that time my country is going to need me.'[9] I have no doubt 9/11 was for Bush that 'something'. He once told the Palestinian Foreign Minister, 'I'm driven with a mission from God. He told me, "George, go and fight those terrorists in Afghanistan." And I did. And he told me, "George, go end the tyranny in Iraq." And I did.'[10] Geoffrey Perret, the biographer among others of Ulysses S. Grant, Abraham Lincoln and Dwight D. Eisenhower, wrote, 'This is the language of no other Commander-in-Chief in American history.'[11] From James Madison until George W. Bush, US Presidents issued 322 'signing statements' to ensure presidential power and prerogatives, an average of eight per President. In his first six years in office, Bush produced nearly 800 in defence of his belief, reinforced by his Vice President Cheney, in the doctrine of the unitary executive and the claim in an emergency to rule by decree.

In relation to hubris it is striking how the role of the divine has been transformed between the world of ancient Greece and our own. In the Greek world the gods represent an inexorable reality that a mere human must not transgress: they warn against hubris and punish it with nemesis. In the world of Bush and Blair, God is the force which drives the hero to challenge reality: hubris is not something to worry about and nemesis is no more than the bad luck all heroes are bound to encounter at some stage on their crusade through this vale of tears. At least they believe they will have their reward in heaven. Kevin Phillips, an American historian who understands Bush's Republican Party, has written: 'Few questions will be more important to the twenty first century United States than whether renascent religion and its accompanying political hubris will be carried on the nation's books as an asset or as a liability.'[12] In 2012 religion looks set to be every bit as important in the Presidential election campaign as it has been in the recent past.

The reason for concentrating on the hubris of Bush and Blair over Iraq is not simply that theirs is the most striking and the most recent example of political leaders succumbing to what I have called hubris syndrome. It is also their unusual link to strong fundamental Christian beliefs. I believe the syndrome should be studied to find out why the condition affects only some heads of government – and leaders in other fields – but not others. It is not in itself a personality syndrome such as the recognised narcissistic personality syndrome, which begins in early adulthood. It is not a condition, usually, which those leaders affected by it bring to office. Rather it appears to develop when heads of government have been in power for a while. Existing personality traits, though, do seem to make some leaders more susceptible to it than others, and factors to do with the severe external or internal stress seem to play a role too.

Against such past and present evidence of the damage that hubris syndrome can do to a leader's rational decision-making, it seems wise not just for classical philosophers, playwrights, anthropologists and historians to study hubris, but for neuroscientists, medical doctors and psychiatrists to investigate hubris syndrome. There is a case for working on the supposition that there is an underlying syndrome in which a combination of signs and features are more likely to appear together than independently, and which may yet be judged by the medical profession as forming a pathological category. I have developed this argument mainly in articles in medical journals subject to peer review. I have also established the Daedalus Trust.[13] which aims to promote research on a multidisciplinary basis into personality changes associated with the exercise of power.

Tony Blair and George Bush's health

At various times both Tony Blair and George Bush have sought to hide their medical history, in this they are not exceptional among heads of government. Secrecy, far from stopping speculation, has encouraged it. We do not know whether any drugs or medication they may have taken in office contributed to them developing hubris syndrome.

Tony Blair's health

Tony Blair, at forty-four, was one of Britain's youngest Prime Ministers when he first came to power in 1997. On Sunday 19 October 2003 it was leaked to the press that Blair had attended Stoke Mandeville Hospital near to Chequers, his official country home. Only later was this news officially confirmed by 10 Downing Street. Blair was then transferred to west London's

Hammersmith Hospital to be treated, allegedly, for only a commonplace increase in his heartbeat. Later that night, when Blair returned to No. 10, it was stated that he had never suffered from heart problems before. But it was also announced that at Hammersmith Hospital he had had cardiac shock treatment, or cardioversion. In as much as a medical condition was named at all, it was referred to as a 'supra-ventricular tachycardia', a term which in this context was ambiguous. It meant either a relatively benign arrhythmia (an abnormality of the heartbeat), or something from a range of arrhythmias not so benign such as atrial fibrillation and atrial flutter, caused when the arrhythmia has its origins above the ventricles.

Some cardiologists were surprised that the Prime Minister had had cardioversion for what was being described merely as a 'supra-ventricular tachycardia' and felt his real condition was likely to be atrial flutter. The suspicion that there might be something more serious about Blair's medical condition was strengthened by Bill Clinton blurting out, 'As soon as I heard what happened I called in to check he was OK. We had a talk and he sounded in good shape. I've known about this for a long time. He told me about it quite a few years ago.'[14] In a later TV documentary, Tina Weaver, editor of the *Sunday Mirror*, described 'being at a restaurant in Barcelona, days after the Prime Minister's heart scare last October', when Clinton arrived. She said:

I told him who I was and asked if he had heard if the Prime

Minister had had a heart scare. He was very relaxed about it and said, yes, he had and indeed had spoken to him. Then he went on to say he wasn't surprised, it was a condition he knew about and in fact the Prime Minister had told him that he suffered from this condition some years earlier and it was brought on by a combination of too little sleep and too much caffeine.[15]

On 27 October a statement was issued from No. 10 to deal with Clinton's claim: 'The Prime Minister did not have, and had never had, a heart condition, nor had he had this complaint before.'[16] Clinton's claim was also flatly contradicted by Blair on BBC Radio 2. Asked whether he had told Clinton that he had a heart condition, Blair said, 'No, this is the first time this has ever happened to me. I'm told it is a relatively common thing to have happened to you and it is a relatively minor treatment.'[17] We now know from the diary of a senior Cabinet minister, David Blunkett, that two days after treatment, 'Tony told me when I spoke to him on the telephone that he had had the heart problem, on and off, for fifteen years, but this time he had to go into hospital, which was why it became public knowledge.'[18]

On 4 November 2003 I talked to Blair at a diplomatic reception and I noted down afterwards that he was clearly very worried and that he had aged very much, deep in his face, the contours of which seemed to have changed. He also appeared to have lost weight. I wondered then if his heart condition had been brought on by increased activity in his thyroid gland, which would have explained his weight loss and hyperactivity, but there is no evidence that thyrotoxicosis was diagnosed. President Bush Sr had been admitted to hospital in May 1991, after he had become unusually tired and short of breath while jogging. He was diagnosed as having atrial fibrillation which later was confirmed as being due to thyrotoxicosis. To his credit all of this was made public at every stage but it was a serious illness and some of its effects were still with him during his ineffective and lacklustre campaign against both Bill Clinton and Ross Perrot later that year.

In December 2003 there were reports of a specialist doctor rushing to No. 10 on a motorbike to treat Blair because he had developed acute stomach pain. Speculation followed that what had provoked this emergency was a suspected attack of appendicitis, but for cardiac experts there was far more concern that it could have been a dreaded, though fortunately not common, complication of atrial flutter – a blood clot forming in the atrium of the heart and throwing off a fragment to become lodged in a vessel supplying the intestines and cutting them off from their oxygen supply. This would cause acute pain. Fortunately this proved to be a false alarm.

The suspicion that Blair was covering up a long-standing heart condition also increased when a journalist working undercover, as a footman, in Buckingham Palace, wrote in the *Daily Mirror* on 20 November 2003 that the Queen had asked a page to delay dinner until she had heard that the Prime Minister's treatment was successful. She was purported to have said to the page, 'He's told me he's had similar complications in the past,' reinforcing Clinton's claim. Downing Street responded to this by repeating, 'The Prime Minister does not have, and never has had, a heart condition.'[19] But one book has claimed that an episode had transpired as early as 1997.[20] This may have stemmed from the report in the *Guardian* on 21 November 2003 that 'a well-placed source from the Prime Minister's Sedgefield constituency claimed that the Labour leader suffered palpitations or a similar condition before the 1997 election and had sought medical treatment in north-east England for a heart ailment when Labour was still in opposition though he believed the problem was not serious.'

It was then suddenly announced, on 1 October 2004, the day after he said he would fight the next election, that Blair had been admitted for a catheter ablation, as a daytime procedure. Blair's doctor described the condition only as an 'irregular heartbeat' but the hospital called it atrial flutter. The likelihood is that the ablation, involving a radio frequency burn in a localised part of the heart, has been completely successful.

There has been speculation that for some years Blair had been on beta-blocking drugs for his heart arrhythmia. I asked the scientist who developed these drugs whether he knew of any long-term side effects that might predispose Blair to hubris in that the normal alerting mechanism in the body to strain and stress was being damped down. He claimed to have had a similar request from the Foreign Office about Saddam Hussein! His answer was that he could not find anyone who has reported studies on the long-term psychological effects of beta-blockers, nor any on their acute psychological effects, but there were plenty of anecdotes. One of his favourites came from a professional concert pianist, who told him how emotionally unbalanced his performances used to be before and after the interval, prior to taking beta-blockers. Before beta-blockers he would play the first half with such passion that, by the interval, he was emotionally exhausted. Going into the second half after a shower and a quick change, he felt emotionally flat. After taking the beta-blocker propranolol he found that he could play the first half in better intellectual control; he no longer felt emotionally drained, giving, for him, a more satisfying second half. The result was a more even performance intellectually. He wasn't sure which experience he preferred or whether the audience noticed! Some years later I addressed the complex questions surrounding these beta-blocking drugs in a lecture at the Institute of Neurology in memory of Professor David Marsden with whom I had done neuroscience research on beta blockers at St Thomas's Hospital in the 1960s. [21]

One doctor wrote to me speculating on the medication Tony Blair might have been taking, that having watched him on TV for many years, he had noticed how his receding hairline had moved forward and then after his announcement of his treat-ment for tachycardia, had moved back again. The doctor wondered whether Blair might have been taking Regaine for hair growth, which has a recorded side effect of triggering tachycardias. He postulated that when the doctors realised he was on Regaine, they told him to stop using it. Whatever the truth, the likelihood is that it is Blair's personality rather than his health that contributed to him developing hubris syndrome.

One investigative journalist labelled all this as 'deceit'. Yet Blair was not the first and will probably not be the last head of government to dissemble over their health. It was, however, emblematic of his tenure at No. 10. 'Neither the falsehood which preceded the invasion of Iraq, nor the lies which followed it, nor the crisis which had resulted, were an accident. They flowed directly from the changed structure of government that was imposed after the victory of New Labour.'[22] His memoirs say a little about his health.[23] He sticks to the position that his arrhythmia only started in 2003 and says of his heart operation in 2004 "I decided to throw so much at the media that they wouldn't quite know what to make of it all, and I gave them three stories at once. I would fight the third election but not the fourth; I had bought a house; I was having a heart operation . . . the house was bought and so was some time."

George W. Bush's health

During the last week of George W. Bush's first presidential campaign, it became known that he had been arrested for driving a car under the influence of alcohol at the age of thirty. Starting in 1999, it had been made fairly clear in unattributable briefings that as a young man the candidate had been too fond of alcohol. This was presented as a passing phase of little consequence; in fact he was an alcoholic. On alcoholism there is no room for complacency. It is a condition that, once it has manifested itself, demands constant vigilance to ensure alcohol abuse does not continue in total secrecy and with the patient in denial.

Since he has been President, records of Bush's medical condition have been published every year by his doctors. On only one occasion was there some delay. They reveal little of interest except that he had an abnormally low pulse rate. Yet for some years Bush has been uttering so many malapropisms that besides making him the butt of many jokes, they have focused doctors' minds on whether or not he has dyslexia, from which his brother Neil is reported to suffer. There has also been speculation on whether Bush has adult attention deficit hyper - activity disorder (ADHD), a life-long disorder characterised by overactive behaviour, short attention span and poor concentration. A further reason for speculation in Bush's case is that there is a well-established association between dyslexia and ADHD. Also ADHD is one of four psychiatric disorders, the others being depression, post-traumatic stress disorder and schizophrenia,[24] which commonly co-occur with substance abuse disorders such as alcoholism.

Bush claims he has drunk no alcohol since 1987, but there have been rumours in the press to the contrary. On 13 January 2002 he lost consciousness while sitting on a couch in the White House watching a football game. His head hit the floor, resulting in an abrasion on his left cheekbone. The incident was blamed on a combination of not feeling well in previous days and an improperly eaten pretzel. I was contacted by a British doctor who had visited Johns Hopkins University and in talking to a group of young doctors was told that, following this incident, though the President had been admitted to Walter Reed Hospital, a blood sample of his had been sent to Johns Hopkins which showed a blood alcohol level in the range of 200mg. All such rumours have been emphatically denied by the White House and certainly there are no signs of Bush resuming his drinking habits in his retirement which he has handled so far with considerable grace and a low key style.

Personality was once thought to play an important role in alcoholism, although it is felt to play a somewhat lesser role today as a contributor to addiction.[25] Yet it is obvious that some people's personalities are part and parcel of their addictive habit and influence whether they overcome their addiction. Bush has never made any secret of the fact that he does not read much and claims that he is no intellectual. But that does not mean – as some assume – that he has a low IQ. While he was a 'C' student, which means he had to rely on the strength of his family connections to get into Yale, he graduated from both Yale Law School and Harvard Business School, which is not possible without a fair amount of intelligence. Some who meet Bush one-on-one claim to be pleasantly surprised by his intelligence. Question marks about Bush relate, therefore, more to his inattention, his incurious nature and inarticulacy: in short, signs that his brain functions in an unusual way.

Armchair   psychiatrists,   according   to   one   American magazine,[26] have for some time argued that Bush suffers from a classic case of narcissistic personality disorder. This, like other personality disorders, begins in early adulthood. Psychoanalytic studies of George Bush offer deeper insights but a warning note needs to be struck for the record of psychoanalysts writing about political leaders whom they have not treated as patients is not good. Freud, for example, wrote a rather bad book about Woodrow Wilson using evidence provided by a colleague of Wilson's. Blair has been the subject of an analytical study by a former Labour MP, Leo Abse[27] which in many ways was rather prescient.

One of the analytical books on Bush is by Dr Justin Frank, who believes that the characteristics of his personality overlap meaningfully with a description of what he defines as a megalomanic state:

> The troubles in Bush's early childhood might have made a megalomanic solution an attractive way to adapt – to cope with, and even triumph over, his circumstances. Both megalomania and mania exhibit three overtly similar defensive characteristics: control, contempt and triumph. Simple mania involves love and the need to deny depen - dency or loss of a loved person; megalomania involves hate and a need to triumph over paranoid fears. A manic person wants to repair the damage he's caused, once he recognises it. He feels guilt. The megalomaniac is indifferent to any damage he caused, because he had a reason for his actions;

he is without guilt or compassion, and incapable of even thinking about making reparation.[28]

The relationship between such a megalomanic disposition and hubris hardly needs spelling out but I am not convinced Bush suffered from megalomania. I prefer the more limited diagnosis of hubris syndrome after 9/11 and starting to wane in his second term and fading out in retirement.

A very interesting analysis of leaders' personality and mental state is provided in a fascinating new book, *A First-Rate Madness*, by Nassir Ghaemi[29] which takes a unique look at how mental illness can strengthen a leader's personality and that one should not always assume that the net effect of mental illness weakens a leader's capacity but rather it can enhance it. Amongst many case studies he writes about George W Bush and Tony Blair.

I believe that it was only in the period after 9/11 that George W. Bush and Tony Blair developed full-blown hubris syndrome. The assessment of Bush by the distinguished biographer of American Presidents, Stephen Graubard, is that 'hubris com - bined with ignorance led Bush the younger to undertake adventures that concealed the more serious problems abroad that ought to have concerned him', and he goes on to write in a footnote, 'The provincialism of American thinking on foreign policy is today replicated in Great Britain.'[30] Lord Morgan, the distinguished biographer of the former Prime Ministers Lloyd George, Ramsay MacDonald and Callaghan, wrote of Blair's appearance at the Labour Party conference after 9/11:

Blair seemed a political colossus, half-Caesar, half-Messiah. Equally, as times became tough following the Iraq *imbroglio*, he became an exposed solitary victim, personally stigmatised as in the 'cash for peerages' affair. Blair discovered, like Lloyd George and Thatcher before him, that British politics do not take easily to the Napoleonic style.[31]

What drove both Bush and Blair into hubris syndrome is not easy to quantify; there are some predisposing factors in their character and perhaps a few medical clues, but nothing that is definite. The fact that both were secretive about their medical history means one has to look deeper but there are no proven linkages.

The last fifty years have seen an explosion of sciences relating to people's mental make-up. Genetics, neuroscience, psychology and epidemiology are all forging ahead and finding new ways of augmenting each other. No scientific explanation of hubristic acts has yet been found and no such explanation may ever be found. However, watching the changes in the new sciences of the mind in my lifetime, as a former neurologist and politician, I believe they may ultimately provide an explanation of why some leaders succumb to hubris syndrome while others do not.[32] It may be that hubris syndrome never has a medical cure or even a proven medical causation, but it is becoming ever clearer that, as much as or even more than conventional illness, it is a great menace to the quality of leadership and the proper government of our world in all its aspects, not just political but particularly financial.

Curbing political leaders' hubristic behaviour, like that of Bush and Blair, has to rely on strengthening the national democratic checks and balances built up over the years in both the USA and the UK. Perhaps the most important is Cabinet vigilance and scrutiny, for those are the people who see the most of their heads of government's true conduct in office. The resignation of Robin Cook in 2003 over Iraq had an impact in the UK although by then he was no longer Foreign Secretary. Had Colin Powell, as Secretary of State, resigned before the Iraqi war – which, given his serious reservations, he was certainly entitled to do – the effect might have been considerable. Yet Bush and Blair respectively won national elections in 2004 and 2005 and in 2006 and 2007, the electorate registered their considerable dissatisfaction, which led to changes in policy but they still elected them. In truth many liked their apparent decisiveness, risk taking and readiness to go to war.

Press criticism was muted in both countries before the Iraq war and for a while afterwards, either because their proprietors agreed with the decision to go to war or the journalists who had predicted a much more difficult military operation initially than proved to be the case, then found themselves for a few months somewhat discredited. It was also difficult for anyone to predict the insurgency without knowing more about the paucity of aftermath planning. But there was far too little investigative journalism about the preparation. Many of us, and I certainly include myself, were too complacent, too trusting in a military, political machinery with which we were familiar, perhaps too familiar, and which had worked well as recently as in 1991.

In a democracy nothing can replace knowing more about the true nature and character of the people we vote in to become head of our government. The importance of character is made clear in the work of James Hillman. In his book *The Force of Character*, he writes: 'The limiting effect of one's innate image prevents that inflation, that trespassing or hubris that the classical world considered the worst of human errors. In this way character acts as a guiding force.'[33] We need more clues, or alerting information, as to why some leaders may develop hubris when in office. The good sense of the people in a democracy is then more likely to ensure that those chosen have qualities in their character which will not succumb to the intoxication of power.

If, as I believe, hubris syndrome is acquired, as I argue earlier, then it is important to assess Bush and Blair now they have ceased to be President and Prime Minister. In the case of Bush the high point of his hubris reached its zenith on USS *Abraham Lincoln* on 1 May 2003 when he spoke in front of a banner declaring "Mission Accomplished". There is some evidence, however, that his hubris began to decline even while in office from 2005, following the removal of Donald Rumsfeld. Bush began to listen and plot a rather different course, deciding to increase substantially US forces on the ground in Iraq as part of the seemingly successful 'surge' strategy. He was generous to

President Obama from the outset and he seems content in retirement in Midland, Texas with only rare public appearances. His memoirs show little sign of hubris and have surprised many for their modest tone.

Tony Blair, by contrast, negotiated in very unusual circumstances, in the last few days of his Prime Ministership, that he would succeed James Wolfensohn, as the Quartet's Special Envoy (US, UN, EU, Russia) charged with promoting Palestinian governance, the economy and security. He also later lobbied very hard to be appointed President of the European Union Council but this was fortunately blocked. Certainly no one reading his memoirs can be under any illusion that Blair still sees himself as a major global figure. In his two appearances before the Iraq Inquiry he seemed to want to divert attention by constantly talking about the threat of Iran developing nuclear weapons. On the eve of the tenth anniversary of 9/11 on Radio 4's *Today* programme he made it pretty clear that he believes the bombing of Iran's nuclear installations was a serious option. There has been little or no readiness to admit serious error over Iraq, even to conceive it possible that he could be mistaken in the real meaning of those words. Based on his performance he will, in the American phrase, continue to "strut his stuff". Blair's memoirs, in stark contrast to those of George W Bush, contain very little serious analysis or admissions of the other choices available to him in relation to the Iraq war. His conduct and demeanour indicate hubris syndrome still dominates.

Nassir Ghaemi, who is Professor of Psychiatry and runs the

Mood Disorder Program at Tufts University, states that Tony Blair in his memoirs indirectly confirms the diagnosis of hubris syndrome by writing, as follows, about himself:

'The difference between the TB of 1997 and the TB of 2007 was this: faced with this opposition across such a broad spectrum in 1997, I would have tacked to get the wind behind me. Now I was not doing it. I was prepared to go full into it if I thought it was the only way to get to my destination. "Being in touch" with opinion was no longer the lodestar. "Doing what was right" had replaced it.'[34]

'But what if you are not right?' laconically asks Nassir Ghaemi. It is hard to avoid the harsh conclusion that Blair has no capacity as yet to distinguish right from wrong in many areas of his past responsibilities.

Conclusions

One of the questions that will shape public attitudes to the Iraq Inquiry is whether they will judge Prime Minister Tony Blair acted 'illegally' by invading Iraq. Bush, according to US law and practice, almost certainly did not. He was covered in large part by a Congressional resolution passed in President Clinton's time authorising the use of force to topple Saddam Hussein. Bush also from the start had US public opinion readier to see linkages between Saddam Hussein and al-Qaeda. He had legal advice which concluded that Saddam Hussein was in material breach of specific UN Resolutions. He exercised his right as Commander-in-Chief to order American forces into action in Iraq in ways which his legal advisers in the US considered was fully compatible with international law and which they believed did not require any further Security Council resolutions. Also the US was not then a signatory to the Treaty on the International Criminal Court and that remains the position though they now cooperate with the ICC.

Blair, by contrast, knew and told me in conversations in 1998 that he risked being thought to have acted contrary to international law if he sought to topple Saddam Hussein. The advice of the Legal Adviser to the Foreign and Commonwealth Office, Michael Wood, was outlined clearly in a letter sent to the Foreign Secretary's office on 6 November 2002. That view was supported by the Deputy Legal Adviser, Elizabeth Wilmshurst who resigned in a letter to Michael Wood on 18 March 2003, made available to the Iraq Inquiry. In it she wrote:

"I regret that I cannot agree that it is lawful to use force against Iraq without a second Security Council resolution to revive the authority given in SCR 678 . . . My views accord with the advice that has been given consistently in this Office before and after the adoption of SCR 1441 and with what the Attorney General gave us to understand was his view prior to his letter of 7 March. (The view expressed in that letter has, of course, changed again into what is now the official line). I cannot in conscience go along with advice – within the Office or to the public or Parliament – which asserts the legitimacy of military action without such a resolution, particularly since an unlawful use of force on such a scale amounts to the crime of aggression; nor can I agree with such action in circumstances which are so detrimental to the international order and the rule of law.

I therefore need to leave the Office; my views on the legitimacy of the action in Iraq would not make it possible for me to continue my role as a Deputy Legal Adviser or my work more generally . . ."

Against these perfectly justified and honourably expressed views is the fact that, just before the war, the Attorney General, Sir Peter Goldsmith, the Government's chief legal adviser, changed his view and decided that the war was lawful. He changed his position close to the invasion after discussions with Tony Blair's advisers and after having talked to the legal advisers to President Bush. He was fully entitled to do this and he wrote a full opinion saying, with qualifications, that it was legal to go to war without the second resolution. This opinion was seen not just by the Prime Minister but also by the Foreign Secretary, Jack Straw, who had allowed, quite rightly, his Legal Adviser full rein to express his views while keeping his own counsel. Straw, however, before the invasion accepted the Attorney General's final position, and not the views of his own legal advisory team. A few other Ministers saw the full opinion – but never the whole Cabinet. The Attorney General's office sent a specific very short letter to the Chief of the Defence Staff, Admiral Sir Michael Boyce, who had requested a formal letter, just before the invasion, saying the military action in Iraq was legal. The Attorney General also presented a shortened version of his detailed memo, which removed some of the qualifications, to Cabinet that supported the Prime Minister's decision to commit UK forces to military action. These issues were then fully debated in the House of Commons and by a substantial majority the Government motion was supported. Yet in that debate the former Foreign Secretary, Robin Cook, argued that the intelligence that he had seen did not justify an invasion.

Blair probably did use all sorts of pressures and political tactics to achieve the legal opinion in the end that he wanted from the Attorney General but in the final analysis due process, legally and democratically, was followed in the UK. In that process Blair did, however, cross the line in terms of Parliamentary conduct. He quite specifically distorted the intelligence information he had to Parliament. The factual intelligence information that he, in his special position, was receiving usually is never quoted. If it is it must be quoted accurately. Blair may have disagreed with that intelligence; he may have believed, sincerely, it was wrong but to use it to Parliament in a way that was designed to mislead and to distort it was a serious contempt of Parliament. But that distortion of due process, however regrettable, did not make the invasion illegal.

An important book published in 2010 entitled *The Rule of Law*, written by Tom Bingham and already referred to, judged that the invasion of Iraq in 2003 was illegal. Bingham was Britain's most senior and distinguished judge at the time of the war, someone whom I had asked in 1977 to inquire into the breaking of UN oil sanctions against Southern Rhodesia. A man whose wisdom and integrity I greatly respected. But I do not believe in the case of the Security Council practice and powers he attached sufficient importance to the discretionary political judgement that underpins Security Council resolutions, the legality of which are established in the UN Charter. The basic text is the UN Charter which prohibits any country from using force against another without the latter's consent. The two exceptions to this are if force is used in self-defence, or if force is authorised by the Security Council under Chapter VII of the Charter. That authorisation is not, however, hemmed around by legal precedent as in a Court of Law.

My own conclusion is that the war in Iraq stretched the true interpretation of the UN Charter far less than NATO's humanitarian intervention on the Serbian territory of Kosovo in 1999. Over Kosovo, there was no UN Security Council Resolution saying that action was necessary "to maintain or restore international peace and security". Had such a Resolution been sought, the Russian Federation made it clear it would exercise its veto. Nevertheless, an advisory opinion of the International Court of Justice requested at Serbia's urging in the UN General Assembly found in June 2010 that Kosovo's declaration of independence in 2003 was not in conflict with international law. On this clear yet narrow-based opinion, Kosovo had been recognised by 85 states by the end of October 2011 but not by all member states of the European Union.

In relation to Iraq, the crucial legal questions all really focus around Resolution 1441 passed by the Security Council in November 2002 which reaffirmed Resolution 678 authorising Member States to "use all necessary means" to uphold and implement its Resolution 660 passed in August 1990 following the invasion of Kuwait and all relevant Resolutions subsequent to Resolution 660. From August 1990 until the invasion of Iraq in 2003, the Security Council had been seized by Iraq and the affairs of that country had been under constant discussion whether over the 'no-fly-zones', the presence or absence of weapons of mass destruction, WMD, or the controversial 'oil for food' programme. To dismiss Resolution 660 and all subsequent ones as in any way irrelevant to what happened in 2003 is unrealistic. Their existence was a constant in Security Council discussions over Iraq. Without them the continuation of the 'no-fly-zones' never specifically authorised would not have taken place. Nor would the air attacks launched by the US and the UK in 1998, undertaken to protect their aircraft from constant missile attack, have taken place.

In the negotiations over Resolution 1141 the US, and to a lesser extent, the UK, had resisted the attempt by France and Russia to link any military action to a new Resolution. The wording in this regard was therefore unclear and contested inside the Security Council. I stress again this is frequent on Security Council Resolutions. Once the Resolution was passed there was no other authority empowered to interpret it other than the Security Council. The Attorney General argued, in his initial opinion, as Bingham put it that "A reasonable case could be made that Resolution 1441 was capable in principle of reviving the authorisation in Resolution 678". But the Attorney General made clear there needed to be "strong factual grounds" for concluding that Iraq had failed to take the final opportunity to comply with all aspects of 1441. When the Security Council discussed compliance, there was again a difference of opinion, so much so that there were not the sufficient votes (nine) to carry the second Resolution that the British Prime Minister had wanted and campaigned for. That was so even if Russia and France had abstained and not exercised their veto along with China. This political reality, though very visible, and very

damaging, internationally and nationally, to Britain's decision
to invade, did not make the invasion illegal.

I have earlier detailed an intervention by France with the US
in Washington to argue against the British second Resolution
ever being put forward. The French throughout warned that
there were insufficient votes to carry it. The French judgement
can, in retrospect, be seen as being informed in that the nine
votes turned out not to be there to support the US and UK. It
was also politically sensible; for dropping the second Resolution
would have allowed the French to do what President Yeltsin had
argued for in the case of Kosovo. Namely, simply to acquiesce in
military action and not vote against and in so doing defuse the
tension in the Security Council. If the French representations
had resulted in the second Resolution being dropped by Britain
it would have meant that Tony Blair would have avoided the
humiliation of it being demonstrated publicly that there was
insufficient support for the second Resolution. It is very clear
from evidence to the Iraq Inquiry that this was Tony Blair's very
personal decision. That he misjudged the Security Council
members' readiness to vote for a second Resolution is beyond
dispute. In my view the manner in which he took that decision
was indicative of hubris syndrome. Yet his misjudgement of
itself did not call in question the British Attorney General's
eventual decision conveyed belatedly and in a much shortened
form to the Cabinet that the invasion was legal.

The legal question that the Security Council alone could have
resolved would have been if the nine members who did not want

the second Resolution were to have put down another resolution stating that there were insufficient factual grounds for believing that Iraq was not complying with Resolution 1441 and neither the US nor the UK had exercised their veto. The Security Council, however, was deadlocked between its fifteen members. Everyone knew that three of their number (France, Russia and China) were likely to veto a second Resolution supporting an invasion and two (US and UK) were likely to veto a Resolution saying there was insufficient evidence that Iraq was not in compliance to justify an invasion. Were the UK to have exercised its veto that would have mobilised more opposition in the eventual vote in the House of Commons, but for the Government motion to lose it would have required the Conservative Party to withhold support and a very considerable number of Labour MPs to change their eventual vote – an unlikely outcome. Once the Attorney General had judged under international law the UK's participation in an invasion of Iraq as legal and the decision was taken to vote in the House of Commons and not rely on the Prime Minister's prerogative over a decision to go to war, the issue became a political judgement. A judgement both as to what was legal, and what was wise, taking account of all the circumstances.

France, under President Chirac, despite bad relations with Tony Blair, was nevertheless not ready to put a resolution forward that would have forced the US and UK to veto. In this, as in many other respects, the Security Council is not a court of law forced to make a decision on a legal case before it. The

Security Council member states make political judgements, often based on realpolitik and not always on a strict legal interpretation of the words of the Charter or on the exact words in any Resolution of the Security Council that is before them. The UN founding fathers deliberately provided for a weighted majority and for five countries to have a veto. For these reasons, the Security Council does not make judgements based on what has increasingly been seen as a developing international law. The world has most recently seen this practical negotiated method of working within the Security Council operating successfully over Libya in 2011. Known differences of approach were managed and compromise language adopted in resolutions. The Security Council, by contrast, in 2003 deliberately chose not to take a view in the case of the invasion of Iraq. There is no international court that has been established to deal with questions of conflict that has a higher authority than a Security Council resolution compatible with the UN Charter passed with the requisite majority. It is the Council which decides if a resolution is still before the Council, whether the issue is one on which the Council is still seized, whether the issue can be revived and whether one resolution has been specifically overruled by the passing of another resolution.

I am well aware that there are many people who genuinely want the Iraq Inquiry to say that Tony Blair acted illegally and some who would wish he could be brought before the International Criminal Court. On 15 October 2002 Jack Straw, as Foreign Secretary, had indeed anticipated this becoming an issue and received from his Legal Adviser an urgent preliminary view of the practical consequences of the UK acting without international legal authority in using force against Iraq, including possible legal consequences in domestic law, in the International Criminal Court (ICC) and the International Court of Justice (ICJ). This view was based on the UK entering into an armed conflict that was clearly unlawful, without respectable legal arguments. But his adviser, Michael Wood, thought it was inconceivable that a government which had on numerous occasions made clear its intention to comply with international law would order troops into a conflict without justification in international law and that his comments were therefore in the realm of extremely theoretical speculation. He stated that the Ministerial Code noted the duty of Ministers to comply with the law, including international law. As to possible offences under the International Criminal Court Act 2002, which covers war crimes, including offences under the Geneva Conventions, he pointed out that offences for which the ICC has jurisdiction would only apply if the UK authorities did not investigate properly and, if appropriate, prosecute. Such offences did not stem from the illegality of the use of force itself (*ius ad bellum*) but related to matters such as unlawful targeting (*ius in bello*). "The legality of the conflict would not therefore be directly in issue, either in our own courts under the Act or in the ICC but the choice of lawful targets would be difficult if the objectives of the conflict were themselves unlawful." He went on to mention that war crimes might need to be investigated by the

UK in order to ensure that the ICC itself did not take jurisdiction. He also warned that while the ICC at present has no jurisdiction over the crime of aggression, since there is such a crime in international law it was conceivable that an attempt might be made in UK domestic courts to launch a private prosecution for the crime of aggression. He also confirmed that the ICJ has jurisdiction over states not over individuals.

I personally cannot envisage the ICC not accepting that the UK Iraq Inquiry is a proper investigation. Were the Inquiry to judge that the UK Government had acted illegally in invading Iraq, which I doubt they will, then it is conceivable though unlikely that Tony Blair would be prosecuted in the UK. Taking account of all these arguments, I cannot personally support the case that Blair acted illegally under the UN Charter. Nevertheless, if the Attorney General had maintained his earlier position that an invasion was illegal and Blair had sought to circumvent it, then an invasion would have been illegal. Parliament if in full knowledge of an Attorney General's dissenting view, would probably not have voted to support an invasion knowing that if it were to do so it would provoke a clash with our unwritten Constitution.

There is mounting evidence already published by the Inquiry that Blair acted imprudently in going ahead with the invasion without full planning for the aftermath. He never put in place the sustained detailed planning undertaken by Prime Minister John Major before the Gulf War in 1991. But imprudence – which in Blair's case can be argued was feckless, even perhaps going as far as being grossly negligent – is not the same as committing an illegal act in going to war. What of the critical decision by Blair not to challenge the opinion of the Chiefs of Staff and to move British troops to Baghdad in May 2003 described earlier. It might be thought to run against Blair having hubris syndrome, but inattention to detail – indeed a disdain for detail as unnecessary and almost unbecoming for a leader focused on the big picture – is often an accompaniment of hubris syndrome. It was a political, as well as a military, choice open to Blair and his Ministerial colleagues. Whether to deploy troops was not, contrary to evidence given to the Inquiry, a purely military decision. Churchill would not have hesitated on an issue like this to make his views clear. On most occasions he would have succeeded in persuading the Chiefs of Staff. But it can be argued that on this occasion there was less hubris present in Blair than on other occasions. But Blair's technique was not so much to override decisions of the experts but to ensure by various means that they were either not heard or sidelined. Just as in his relations with Gordon Brown he tended not to confront but to circumvent. On this occasion he neither circumvented or countermanded but acquiesced with huge consequences.

What Blair did in Government particularly from 2001 onwards was to create a climate of decision making inside No. 10 which was without precedent in downgrading Cabinet government and downgrading military, civil service, diplomatic and intelligence advice. This was definitely hubristic. The effect this had was well illustrated by an obviously frustrated adviser,

Major General Michael Laurie, emailing Sir John Chilcot on 27 January 2010 to comment on the position taken by Alastair Campbell during his evidence to the Inquiry on 12 January 2010. His email objected to Campbell having stated to the Inquiry that the purpose of the Dossier was not to make a case for war. "I and those involved in its production saw it exactly as that, and that was the direction we were given." He went on to write in the same email, "During the drafting of the Dossier every fact was managed to make it as strong as possible, the 'final' statements reaching beyond the conclusions intelligence assessment would normally draw from such facts. It was clear to me that there was direction and pressure being applied on the JIC and its drafters."

We know about the atmosphere in No. 10 Downing Street from published evidence to the Inquiry from MI6 officers. One referred to as SIS 2, regarded Alastair Campbell as "somewhat of an unguided missile" with a "propensity to have rushes of blood to the head". It was stated that MI6 was "too eager to please". Also that there was a "very febrile atmosphere" surrounding decisions and that they were "cutting corners". It was stated "I think perhaps SIS was at that point guilty of flying too close to the sun". An officer, SIS 1, admitted on its claim that chemical weapons could be fired within 45 minutes referred to by Prime Minister Blair in the first dossier, "I think we marketed that intelligence . . . before it was fully validated". When reading the Inquiry evidence, with my own direct knowledge of how the Cabinet and the JIC were handled by Prime Minister Harold

Wilson from 1968-70; by James Callaghan from 1977-79; and by John Major over the former Yugoslavia from 1992-1995, I have no doubt this JIC was rendered dysfunctional and acted inappropriately. But something far worse happened. Blair quoted intelligence material to Parliament incorrectly.

His claim that Saddam Hussein could develop a nuclear weapon in 'between one and two years' and that this claim was based on a judgement of the intelligence community, has never been properly authenticated and I repeat, the Cabinet Office has admitted after a Freedom of Information Act request that it does not hold any such information.

In a devastating intervention in the House of Lords, on 22 February 2007, Butler spoke for the first time as an individual, not as the chairman of a Report on Intelligence during the Iraq war.[1] He accused Blair of being 'disingenuous' about the intelligence, saying:

> Here was the rub: neither the United Kingdom nor the United States had the intelligence that proved conclusively that Iraq had those weapons. The Prime Minister was disingenuous about that. The United Kingdom intelligence community told him on 23 August 2002 that we 'know little about Iraq's chemical and biological weapons work since late 1988'. The Prime Minister did not tell us that. Indeed, he told Parliament only just over a month later that the picture painted by our intelligence services was 'extensive, detailed and authoritative'. Those words

could simply not have been justified by the material that the intelligence community provided to him.

The use of the word 'disingenuous' was a very serious allegation, largely ignored by the media and Parliament.

On Thursday, 3 June 2010 at a private morning session of the Inquiry[2] Major General Michael Laurie, Head of intelligence collection for Defence Intelligence (DIS) at the material time was closely examined by the Inquiry members on what he had written in January on the position taken by Alastair Campbell during his evidence. It needs to be borne in mind that an earlier draft of the dossier had been prepared in February and March and had been rejected, Laurie assumed, because it did not make a strong enough case and he had felt under pressure to find intelligence that could reinforce the case. He said in oral evidence, "We were reporting on what we could find and were being asked the whole time, "Can you not find more? Why can't you find more?", and I think there was an assumption that there was stuff there but we were not capable of finding it. I mean the answers were, in a way, exactly as I've said: you can only see what is there."

Sir Roderic Lyne also questioned Laurie about WMD:.. the trailers that Colin Powell showed in his evidence to the UN in 2003 in February, which were not very clear, ******* [redaction]

Major General Michael Laurie: ***********. I don't recall us ever definitively from our side being able to say, "Those are BW production trailers". [BW = biological weapons]

Sir Roderic Lyne: And then CW, what would you see there? [CW = chemical weapons]

Major General Michael Laurie: I mean almost the same – I mean the same answer really. It's production facilities and activity at them.

Sir Roderic Lyne: Now if we move into bigger stuff: nuclear. If there was a significant programme of developing nuclear weaponry, presumably that would leave a much bigger trace?

Major General Michael Laurie: [response heavily redacted].

The Chairman (Sir John Chilcot) went on to ask Laurie about other aspects of his concerns: Are we talking semantics here?

Major General Michael Laurie: I think we are, yes, we are talking semantics here.

The Chairman: But your concern in sending us a submission was that you thought that Alistair Campbell's evidence mis - represented things?

Major General Michael Laurie: Well, I think behind my concern is the line that "we read the intelligence and made a decision on that and then the intelligence turned out to be wrong" and I don't think that is fair. The intelligence in JIC papers was balanced and cautious. The dossier was more certain and therefore to imply that things put in the dossier were wrong because of the certainty expressed in the dossier is not fair to the intelligence people.

The Chairman: Again, you will have read the Butler committee – on which I sat – account. Do you broadly accept that analysis in the Butler report?

Major General Michael Laurie: Yes, yes I do.

The Chairman: – that nuances were lost, the intelligence was asked to bear more weight than it could, but nonetheless there was not actually physical disjunction between JIC assessments on the one hand and the contents of the dossier, as opposed to, perhaps, the foreword?

Major General Michael Laurie: No, I agree with that, I agree with that. But people should make decisions based on the JIC assessments not on a dossier for public presentation.

The Chairman: I've got two other points, if I may, on the dossier before we move on. One is the foreword and its relationship to the contents of the dossier. One can argue angels on pinheads about the content and its relationship to the stream of JIC assessments. The foreword is a different document and John Scarlett in evidence has in a sense disowned responsibility for the content and language of the foreword. When they eventually published, did the language of the foreword create real concern among your colleagues and indeed in your own mind? It talks about "beyond doubt" and so on.

Major General Michael Laurie: . . . at the time I do recall being – not very concerned, but noting that the missile test bed we described in the dossier we described as "new" and it was new but it wasn't working, so the word "new" sort of implied "this is just about ready to go". But it wasn't – one sort of said it is not important in itself and it doesn't matter because the JIC papers did actually describe it properly.

The Chairman: – certainly in the one headline in a news -

paper. It must have been very clear within the DIS that this was about a tactical battlefield weapon and a deployment period from stocks held quite close to front line to deployment, none of which of course is brought out in the dossier. If it had been, would you have been less unhappy?

Then Sir Roderic Lyne took up the Prime Minister's foreword to the document published on 24 September 2002 to Parliament entitled *Iraq's Weapons of Mass Destruction: The Assessment of the British Government* where the Prime Minister, Tony Blair, wrote:

"In recent months, I have been increasingly alarmed by the evidence from inside Iraq that despite sanctions, despite the damage done to his capability in the past, despite the UN Security Council Resolutions expressly outlawing it, and despite his denials, Saddam Hussein is continuing to develop WMD, and with them the ability to inflict real damage upon the region, and the stability of the world."

"Gathering intelligence inside Iraq is not easy. Saddam's is one of the most secretive and dictatorial regimes in the world. So I believe people will understand why the Agencies cannot be specific about the sources, which have formed the judgements in this document, and why we cannot publish everything we know. We cannot, of course, publish the detailed raw intelligence. I and other Ministers have been briefed in detail on the intelligence and are satisfied as to its authority. I also want to pay tribute to our

Intelligence and Security Services for the often extraordinary work that they do."

"What I believe the assessed intelligence has established beyond doubt is that Saddam has continued to produce chemical and biological weapons, that he continues in his efforts to develop nuclear weapons, and that he has been able to extend the range of his ballistic missile programme. I also believe that, as stated in the document, Saddam will now do his utmost to try to conceal his weapons from UN inspectors."

"The picture presented to me by the JIC in recent months has become more not less worrying. It is clear that, despite sanctions, the policy of containment has not worked sufficiently well to prevent Saddam from developing these weapons."

"I am in no doubt that the threat is serious and current, that he has made progress on WMD, and that he has to be stopped."

"Saddam has used chemical weapons, not only against an enemy state, but against his own people. Intelligence reports make clear that he sees the building up of his WMD capability, and the belief overseas that he would use these weapons, as vital to his strategic interests, and in particular his goal of regional domination. And the document discloses that his military planning allows for some of the WMD to be ready within 45 minutes of an order to use them."

Sir Roderic Lyne: . . . The sentence in the foreword that Sir John alluded to, can I just read it to you and then ask you as an intelligence professional to say how you would characterise it? This is from the Prime Minister's foreword: [quoted above.]

"What I believe the assessed intelligence has established beyond doubt is that Saddam has continued to produce chemical and biological weapons, that he continues in his efforts to develop nuclear weapons and that he has been able to extend the range of his ballistic missile programme."

Now, was that a justifiable encapsulation?

Major General Michael Laurie: No, because I don't believe it was beyond doubt. I suppose there were three bits to that. I mean, first of all, there was the language used by Saddam, who I think probably liked to portray that he was more capable than he was. There were clear intentions, both historical and fairly recent at the time, of their wish to have these capabilities, but neither the inspection teams nor ourselves really found a lot of evidence that this stuff was being produced. So capabilities and intentions are very different things and there was no doubt about the intentions –

The Chairman: Confirmed by the ISG after the event.

Major General Michael Laurie: Confirmed, yes, but there was certainly doubt about capabilities. So I think, yes, I mean that's the case.

Sir Roderic Lyne: So "continuing production of chemical and biological, continuing efforts to develop nuclear"; now if you had been the chairman of the JIC and this had been shown to you in draft, would you have queried that sentence?

Major General Michael Laurie: As an intelligence officer, yes I would.

Sir Roderic Lyne: Yes.

Major General Michael Laurie: Yes, I mean one has to have courage and stand up and say "I can't sign up to that", yes.

From this extracted exchange it is clear that having cleverly teased out the full facts when the Iraq Inquiry comes out, they may not focus their criticism on the JIC reports, nor even on the body of the dossier. They may focus their criticism, rightly, in my view, on what the Prime Minister, Tony Blair, wrote in the foreword to the dossier presented to Parliament and to the public. It will be interesting what word they may be prepared to use. I hope, if they believe it, they will say that Blair "lied" to the House of Commons and not choose the word that Lord Butler used in the House of Lords, "disingenuous" which has the same meaning but which does not have the same power to shock. They may, however, find another word to express the public's indignation. Unlike parliamentarians they are not obliged to find terms acceptable in the House of Commons. Churchill once described a lie as a "terminological inexactitude" in deference to the successive Speaker's rulings that the word "lie" cannot be used on the floor of the Chamber. What the members of the Inquiry are obliged to do – if they are not to give the impression of a complete whitewash – is to follow up their assessment, already clear from the evidence, that the Prime Minister misled the House of Commons in both the dossier published to Parliament and on the floor of the House of Commons and then they must assess the gravity of such behaviour. Having no parliamentarians on the Inquiry there are worrying signs that they may not see the importance of this to the proper functioning of our democracy.

We all recognise there are different types of lies. White lies. Grey lies. Sexual lies. Necessary lies. For example, a Chancellor of the Exchequer denying to the House of Commons that they were about to devalue, is acceptable. Even so Jim Callaghan was adamant that having done that in 1967 he should not continue as Chancellor but was persuaded by Wilson to become Home Secretary. During war, no responsible politician will say anything or confirm anything that will endanger the lives of those fighting and this form of lying is understood. But there are black lies, lies that debauch the standards of public life and they must be treated with the utmost seriousness. Public disillusionment has reached a point of thinking and seeing politics as the art of lying. Yet if lies really become the currency of political debate then democracy is endangered. Truth is built on facts. Distort the facts, even if there is no intention to do so, then one has lied.

I wrote to the Chairman of the Iraq Inquiry on 17 November 2009 that in my contact with Parliamentarians many were unaware of Lord Butler's claim in the House of Lords that "the Prime Minister was disingenuous". I asked the Iraq Inquiry to establish five points relating to Lord Butler's speech so that the country could not witness yet another cover up.

When Lord Butler knew that the intelligence community had told Tony Blair that "we know little about Iraq's chemical and biological weapons work since late 1998".

If that information was known to Lord Butler before 14 July 2004 and why, if so, it was not detailed in the Inquiry's Report?

When the chairman of the Iraq Inquiry, Sir John Chilcot, then a member of Lord Butler's Inquiry, was aware that Tony Blair had been told this information.

Whether the late Robin Cook, who consulted the intelligence community prior to his resignation from the Cabinet, was given the same information as had been told to Tony Blair?

Whether Gordon Brown was ever told the same information as Tony Blair, and if so when and when did he first hear about Lord Butler's revelations that Tony Blair had been "disingenuous"?

Sir John Chilcot eventually replied on 13 July 2010:

"I know from your earlier letter that you are interested to know whether Lord Butler's judgement, as expressed in the debate on 22 February 2007, was his private view at the end of his Inquiry; whether he came to that conclusion two years later in the light of re-examination of the evidence already given to his Inquiry; or whether it was because of new evidence. I think I can say that it would not be necessary to call Lord Butler to give evidence to answer that question. At Annex b of the Butler Report there is a table that compares specific aspects of relevant

JIC reports to the corresponding parts of the Government's September Dossier, and to the Foreword to that Dossier by the then Prime Minister. At the bottom of page 165 the quote from the 21 August 2002 JIC paper reads "Although we have little intelligence on Iraq's CBW doctrine, and know little about Iraq's CBW work since 1998, we judge it likely that Saddam would order the use of CBW against coalition forces at some point.." I am sure that it was to this JIC paper that Lord Butler was referring when he said that Mr Blair had been told on 23 August of this judgement but had not told Parliament what the intelligence community had told him."

"As you will have gathered by the publication of the list of witnesses we are to see before the end of July, we have not called Lord Butler."

I also wrote to the Chairman of the Inquiry on 6 October 2010.

"In Brian Jones's recent book *Failing Intelligence*[3] he reports on pages 65 and 66 that Tony Blair on 3 April 2002 on NBC news said "We know that he (Saddam) has stockpiles of major amounts of chemical and biological weapons." Yet according to Mr Jones "The JIC had stated unequivocally on 15 March in an assessment that went to the Prime Minister that it did not have a clear picture of Iraq's WMD and that any stocks it did have were likely to be small." Jones goes on to say "Blair was not to stretch the truth quite so far in future."

Your Committee may already have been made aware of this and you may even be able to draw to my attention, as you did before, to some obscure reference to this information in the Butler Report. But even so it makes it even harder to explain your Committee's decision not to enquire from Lord Butler why these two highly relevant findings were not given more prominence in his Report. It also will open up your Committee to the justifiable charge of a "cover up" if you do not yourselves deal with these two documented issues in your Report.

On page 144 Jones writes, "But his (Blair's) assertion to Hutton that 'Saddam is continuing to develop WMD' which can 'inflict real damage upon the region and the stability of the world' is neither substantiated nor explained anywhere in the dossier or in any of the JIC assessments he received."

A confirmation of Jones's professional assessment came, he claims, in pages 96-98, from a delegation from an unnamed country given a presentation in the Cabinet Office. Have your Committee in your recent foreign visits talked to the experts from that country and will this issue be covered in your report?"

There are some fundamental questions that the Iraq Inquiry seems not to want to ask as to why Lord Butler, two years after his Report was published, felt it necessary to speak out in such a deliberate and pointed way as he did in the House of Lords. Either new information had come to light or Butler felt unable to say in the collective Report what he really felt. The Inquiry should uphold the vital importance of maintaining the principle that a proven lie on a substantive matter to Parliament is as serious as to lie to a Court of Law. Particularly so in matters relating to intelligence, whether quoting or drawing on secret information in support of a policy in what is said in the House of Commons. There is a natural and healthy instinct across the party political divide to believe the words of a Prime Minister, Foreign Secretary or Defence Secretary when speaking on intelligence matters or quoting from intelligence material. That century-long spirit of bipartisanship in international affairs has been gravely damaged by Blair's handling of many issues involving the military invasion of Iraq by the UK in 2003. If lessons are to be learnt, and I hope they will be, it is vital for the Iraq Inquiry to establish whether Lord Butler's words are a fair and true summary of the situation.

The Inquiry has a strange composition in that no one chosen as a member of the Inquiry has ever served in Parliament or Cabinet. This contrasts with the Dardanelles Commission and the Franks Inquiry into the Argentine invasion of the Falklands, both of which included parliamentarians. In the case of the latter, the Franks Inquiry, there was also the fullest consultation by the Prime Minister, Margaret Thatcher, with the Leader of the Opposition at that time, Michael Foot. Two former Labour Cabinet Ministers, Merlyn Rees and Harold Lever, served on the Inquiry, together with Anthony Barber and Harold Watkinson, former Conservative Cabinet Ministers.

Contempt of Parliament is a very serious offence punishable within Parliament and it led to the resignation of John Profumo, the Minister in charge of the Army, in 1963. The reason is similar to contempt of Court, for which the legal system takes the criminal offence of perjury very seriously to maintain the integrity of its proceedings. So it is for Parliament.

Once Sir Anthony Eden was known to have lied on the floor of the House of Commons on 20 December 1956, well after the invasion was over, by saying "there was not foreknowledge that Israel would attack Egypt" many Members of the House of Commons from all parties knew he had to resign as Prime Minister. This he did on 10 January 1957 claiming health reasons but this was not the main reason though his health was in large part an explanation for his conduct.[4]

Having stepped down under the political pressure from the Labour Party in 2007, Tony Blair did not stay a Member of Parliament. He also decided not to become a member of the House of Lords. He is, therefore, no longer strictly accountable in Parliament. It would be a travesty of the Iraq Inquiry evidence if they did not judge the former Prime Minister, Tony Blair, for what he said to Parliament. In the case of Eden, there was a medical explanation for his conduct. In Blair's case the explanation I have tried to demonstrate rests within the concept of hubris syndrome. The best formulation for the Inquiry if they believe his foreword was untrue, might be to declare Blair guilty of contempt of Parliament. That simple, but telling, verdict would be a sufficient penalty I suspect for most fair minded people in the country and if Blair challenged the verdict of the Inquiry through spin and evasion it could be confirmed by a motion passed in both Houses of Parliament.

Many know Lord Acton's famous dictum, 'Power tends to corrupt, and absolute power corrupts absolutely.' But Acton preceded that with a plea to judge those who hold power by a higher standard than those who do not: 'I cannot accept your canon that we are to judge Pope and King unlike other men, with a favourable presumption that they did no wrong. If there is any presumption it is the other way against the holders of power.'

Notes

Prologue

1. My original book *In Sickness and in Power: Illness in Heads of Government during the Last 100 Years* was published by Methuen in the spring of 2008 with an updated paperback version in the spring of 2011.

2. Bertrand Russell, *A History of Western Philosophy*, 2nd ed. (London: George Allen & Unwin, 1961), p. 782.

3. Plato, *Phaedrus*, 238a, in *Euthyphro/Apology/Crito/Phaedo/Phaedrus*, tr. H. N. Fowler, Loeb Classical Library (Cambridge, MA: Harvard University Press, 1914); the Ancient Greek original has been added in italics by the author of this book.

4. *Aristotle, Art of Rhetoric*, tr. J. H. Freese, Loeb Classical Library (Cambridge, MA: Harvard University Press, 1926), 1378b.

5. David E. Cooper, *The Measure of Things: Humanism, Humility, and Mystery* (Oxford: Clarendon Press, 2002), p. 163.

6. Margaret Canovan, 'Hannah Arendt as a Conservative Thinker', in Larry May and Jerome Kohn (eds), *Hannah Arendt: Twenty Years On* (Cambridge, MA: MIT Press, 1996), p. 29.

7. Ian Kershaw, *Hitler 1889–1936: Hubris* (London: Allen Lane, 1998); Ian Kershaw, *Hitler 1936–1945: Nemesis* (London: Allen Lane, 2000).

8. David Owen, *Time To Declare* (Penguin paperback edition 1992), p.732.

9. Howard S. Schwartz, 'Narcissism Project and Corporate Decay: The Case of General Motors', *Business Ethics Quarterly* (1991), vol. 1, no. 3.

10. Gerald Russell, 'Psychiatry and politicians: the "hubris syndrome": http://pb.rcpsych.org/cgi/reprint/35/4/140.pdf Lord David Owen, 'Psychiatry and politicians – afterword: Commentary on . . . Psychiatry and politicians': http://pb.rcpsych.org/cgi/reprint/35/4/145.pdf Lawrence Freedman, 'Mental states and political decisions: Commentary on . . . Psychiatry and politicians': http://pb.rcpsych.org/cgi/reprint/35/4/148.pdf

11 Cools R, Sheridan M, Jacobs E, D'Esposito M. 'Impulsive personality

predicts dopamine-dependent changes in frontostriatal activity during component processes of working memory.' *J of Neuroscience* 2007; 27: 5506-14.

12 Lidstone Sarah C et al. 'Effects of Expectation on Placebo-Induced Dopamine Release in Parkinson's Disease.' *Arch. Gen Psychiatry*/Vol 67 (No 8) August 2010.

13. www.daedalustrust.org.uk

14. David Owen. *Time To Declare: Second Innings* (London: Politico's, 2009) p.602-3.

The hubris syndrome

1. Oliver Harvey, *The War Diaries of Oliver Harvey*, ed. John Harvey (London: Collins, 1978).

2. John Connell, *Auchinleck: A Biography of Field-Marshal Sir Claude Auchinleck* (London: Cassell, 1959).

3. Roy Jenkins, *Churchill* (London: Macmillan, 2001), p. 737.

4. David Owen, 'Winston Churchill and Franklin Roosevelt: Did their health problems impair their effectiveness as world leaders', Churchill Lecture, Cabinet War Rooms, 5 May 2009.

5. Mary Soames, *Clementine Churchill* (London: Cassell, 1979), p.291.

6a. Robert Dallek, *An Unfinished Life: John F. Kennedy 1917–1963* (Boston: Little, Brown, 2003).

6b. Jonathan R T Davidson, Kathryn M Connor, Marvin Swartz, 'Mental Illness in US Presidents between 1776 and 1974', *The Journal of Nervous and Mental Disease*, Vol 194, No 1, January 2006.

6c. David Owen, 'The Effect of Prime Minister Anthony Eden's Illness on his Decision-Making during the Suez Crisis', *QJM*, vol. 98, pp. 387–402.

7. Ibid, Davidson, Connor and Swartz, pp. 47–51.

8. Raymond Moley, quoted in Bert Edward Park, *The Impact of Illness on World Leaders* (Philadelphia: University of Pennsylvania Press, 1986), pp. 280–1. Moley was a political science professor from Cleveland taken on as a speech writer by Roosevelt when he decided to run for governor of New York in 1928. On 24 June 1936 Roosevelt had a row with Moley over his criticism of the President in *Today* magazine and this marked the end of their friendship.

9. Shesol Jeff, *Supreme Power: Franklin Roosevelt vs The Supreme Court* (New York: W W Norton, 2010), p.239.

10. Ibid, Shesol, p. 507.

11. Ibid, Shesol, pp. 249-250.

12. David Owen, *In Sickness and In Power* (London: Methuen, 2008), p. 18.

13. George Bush and Brent Scowcroft, *A World Transformed* (New York: Alfred A. Knopf, 1998), p. 249.
14. Hugo Young, *This Blessed Plot: Britain and Europe from Churchill to Blair* (London: Macmillan, 1998), pp. 367 & 368.
15. David Owen, *Time to Declare* (London: Michael Joseph, 1991), p. 777.

Bush, Blair and the war in Iraq
1. Jerrold M. Post (ed.), *The Psychological Assessment of Political Leaders: With Profiles of Saddam Hussein and Bill Clinton* (Ann Arbor: University of Michigan Press, 2003), p. 344.
2. Pierre Rentchnick, *Médecine et Hygiène*, 6 March 1991, p. 662.
3. Hugh L'Etang, *Ailing Leaders in Power 1914–1994* (London: Royal Society of Medicine, 1995), p. 66.
4. Robert Fisk, *The Great War for Civilisation: The Conquest of the Middle East* (London: Fourth Estate, 2005), p. 262.
5. Jonathan C. Randal, *Kurdistan: After Such Knowledge, What Forgiveness?* (London: Bloomsbury, 1988), p. 73.
6. John Kampfner, *Blair's Wars* (London: Free Press, 2003), p. 32.
7. Michael Gordon and Bernard Trainor, *Cobra II: The Inside Story of the Invasion and Occupation of Iraq* (New York: Pantheon / London: Atlantic, 2006), p. 13.
8. Charles Guthrie, 'The war of the generals', *Sunday Times*, 28 March 1999.
9. Bob Woodward, *State of Denial: Bush at War, Part III* (New York: Simon & Schuster, 2006), pp. 60–1.
10. Andrew Rawnsley, *Servants of the People: The Inside Story of New Labour* (London: Hamish Hamilton, 2000), p.272.
11. Kampfner, *Blair's Wars*, p. 49 and p. 57.
12. S. Schachter and J. Singer, 'Cognitive, Social and Physiological Determinants of Emotional State', *Psychological Review* (1962), pp. 69, 379–399.
13. Francis Beckett, 'Blair's Way', *Management Today*, 1 March 2005.
14. Jonathan Powell, *The New Machiavelli: How to Wield Power in the Modern World* (The Bodley Head, 2010).
15. David Owen, 'Two-Man Government', *Prospect*, December 2003; David Owen, 'The Ever-Growing Dominance of No. 10 in British Foreign Policy since 5 April 1982', in Graham Ziegner (ed.), *British Diplomacy: Foreign Secretaries Reflect* (London: Politico's, 2007).
16. David Marquand, 'A man without history', *New Statesman*, 7 May 2007.
17. 'The Secret World of Whitehall Part 2. Behind the Black Door', presented by Michael Cockerill, transmitted on BBC 2, 9 September 2011.

18. Ron Suskind, *The Price of Loyalty: George W. Bush, The White House, and the Education of Paul O'Neill*, pb ed. (New York: Simon & Schuster, 2004), p. 85.

19. George W Bush, *Decision Points* (New York: Crown Publishers, 2010), p.14.

20. Ibid., p. 140 and p. 142.

21. General Sir Rupert Smith, *The Utility of Force: The Art of War in the Modern World* (London: Allen Lane, 2005).

22. Bruce Riedel, 'Al-Qaeda Strikes Back', *Foreign Affairs*, May/June 2007.

23. Louise Richardson, *What Terrorists Want: Understanding the Enemy, Containing the Threat* (New York: Random House, 2006).

24. Kampfner, *Blair's Wars*, p. 263.

25. Leaked memorandum of 29 April 2000 from Tony Blair to staff, reported in *The Times*, 18 July 2000.

26. David Marquand, 'A man without history', *New Statesman*, 7 May 2007.

27. Paul Scott, *Tony & Cherie: A Special Relationship* (London: Sidgwick & Jackson, 2005).

28. Christopher Meyer, *DC Confidential: The Controversial Memoirs of Britain's Ambassador to the U.S. at the Time of 9/11 and the Iraq War* (London: Weidenfeld & Nicolson, 2006), p. 190.

29. Richard A. Clarke, *Against All Enemies: Inside America's War on Terror* (New York: Free Press, 2004), pp. 30–2.

30. Richardson, *What Terrorists Want*, p. 96.

31. Christian Alfonsi, *Circle in the Sand: Why We Went Back to Iraq* (New York: Doubleday, 2006), p. 354.

32. Ibid., pp. 368–9.

33. George Tenet, *At the Center of the Storm: My Years at the CIA* (New York: HarperCollins, 2007), pp. 160 & 255.

34. Thomas E. Ricks, *Fiasco: The American Military Adventure in Iraq* (London: Allen Lane, 2006), p. 31, quoting the National Security Council summary of the conversation reported by the 9/11 Commission.

35. Donald Rumsfeld, *Known and Unknown: A Memoir* (New York: Sentinel, 2011) p. 418 & 425.

36. Tenet, *At the Center of the Storm*, p. 321.

37. H. D. S. Greenway, 'Fatal combination of hubris and incompetence', *Boston Globe*, 3 September 2003; Jonathan Freedland, 'The blind prophet', *Guardian*, 3 September 2003; Arthur Schlesinger Jr, 'Opportunity knocks', *American Prospect*, 21 November 2004; Charles A. Kupchan and Ray Takeyh, 'Middle East: reaping what Bush sowed', *International Herald Tribune*, 19 July 2006; Ricks, Fiasco.

38. Alfonsi, *Circle in the Sand*, p. 68.

39. Ibid., pp. 89 and 115–20.

40. Gordon and Trainor, *Cobra II*, pp. 500–1.

41. George Packer, *The Assassin's Gate: America in Iraq* (New York: Farrar, Straus & Giroux, 2005), p. 147.

42. Mark Danner, *The Secret Way to War: The Downing Street Memo and the Iraq War's Buried History* (New York: New York Review Books, 2006).

43. Ibid., p. 140.

44. David Owen, 'Next stop Iraq', *Wall Street Journal*, 15 November 2001.

45. 'Fall of a Vulcan', *Time*, 7 November 2005.

46. Brian Jones, *Failing Intelligence: the true story of how we were fooled into going to war in Iraq* (London: Dialogue, 2010) pp. 64-5.

47. Danner, *The Secret Way to War*, pp. 148–9.

48. Ibid., pp. 152–3 & 161.

49. Ibid., pp. 88–9.

50. Tenet, *At the Center of the Storm*, p. 310.

51. Danner, *The Secret Way to War*, p. 91.

52. Barbara W Tuchman, *March of Folly: From Troy to Vietnam* (New York: Ballantine, 1985), pp. 374-6.

53. Charles Tripp, 'Militias, vigilantes, death squads', *London Review of Books*, 25 January 2007.

54. Donald Rumsfeld, *Known and Unknown: A Memoir* (New York: Sentinel, 2011), pp. 452-3.

55. George Packer, *The Assassins' Gate*, pp. 114–15.

56. Ahmed Rashid, 'NATO's failure portends a wider war', *International Herald Tribune*, 1 December 2006.

57. John Newhouse, *Imperial America: The Bush Assault on the World Order* (New York: Albert A. Knopf, 2003), p. 43.

58. David Fromkin, *A Peace to End All Peace: The Fall of the Ottoman Empire and the Creation of the Modern Middle East* (New York: Avon, 1990).

59. David Owen, *In Sickness and In Power: Illness in Heads of Government during the last 100 years* (London: Methuen revised edition, 2011) pp. 13-19.

60. Meyer, *DC Confidential*, p. 282.

61. Philippe Sands, *Lawless World: Making and Breaking Global Rules* (Penguin, 2006), pp. 272–3.

62. Don Van Natta Jr, 'Bush was set on path to war, memo by British adviser', *New York Times*, 27 March 2006.

63. Norman Dixon, *On the Psychology of Military Incompetence* (London: Jonathan Cape, 1976), pp. 399–400.

64. Tony Blair, *A Journey* (London: Hutchinson, 2010) pp. 433-4.
65. Michael Isikoff and David Corn, *Hubris: The Inside Story of Spin, Scandal, and the Selling of the Iraq War* (New York: Crown, 2006), p. 419.
66. Meyer, *DC Confidential*, p. 224.
67. Rajiv Chandrasekaran, *Imperial Life in the Emerald City: Inside Baghdad's Green Zone* (London: Bloomsbury, 2007), pp. 31–4.
68. George W Bush, *Decision Points* (New York: Crown, 2010) p. 268.
69. Bob Woodward, *Bush at War* (New York: Simon & Schuster, 2002), pp. 33–4.
70. Charles Cogan, *French Negotiating Behaviour: Dealing with La Grande Nation* (Washington, DC: United States Institute of Peace Press, 2003), pp. 205–9.
71. Tom Bingham, *The Rule of Law* (London: Allen Lane, 2010), p.122-127
72. Sands, *Lawless World*, p. 273.
73. 'Blair's Mission Impossible: the doomed effort to win a second UN Resolution', Comment and Analysis, *Financial Times*, 29 May 2003.
74. Van Natta, 'Bush was set on path to war'.
75. Bob Woodward, *Plan of Attack* (New York: Simon & Schuster, 2004), p. 285.
76. Ned Temko, 'Blair "ignored Chirac on Iraq"', *Observer*, 25 February 2007, reporting on Sir Stephen Wall's interview in a BBC2 three-part documentary on Tony Blair by Michael Cockerell.
77. Ibid.
78. John Vicour, 'A very different take on France's role in Iraq', *International Herald Tribune*, 20 March 2007.
79. Sands, *Lawless World*, Appendix X, pp. 328–342.
80. Ibid., p. 59.
81. Tony Blair, *A Journey* (London: Hutchinson, 2010), p. 436
82. Ibid., p. 435
83. 'Kosovo: The Financial Management of Military Operations', *NAO Report*, 5 June 2000, p. 29.
84. Tony Blair, *A Journey*, pp. 235–243.
85. Strobe Talbott, *The Russian Hand. A Memoir of Presidential Diplomacy* (New York: Random House, 2002).
86. Isikoff and Corn, *Hubris*, op. cit.
87. David Hare, *Stuff Happens* (London: Faber & Faber, 2004).
88. Suskind, *Price of Loyalty*, pp. 127 and 149.
89. Woodward, *State of Denial*, pp. 237–8.
90. Peter W. Galbraith, *The End of Iraq: How American Incompetence Created a War without End* (New York: Simon & Schuster, 2006), p. 102.

91. Chandrasekaran, *Imperial Life in the Emerald City*, p. 77.
92. *Guardian*, 2 May 2007.
93. Chandrasekaran, p. 82.
94. Anthony Seldon, *Blair Unbound* (Simon & Schuster, 2007), p. 191.
95. Tony Blair, *Today*, BBC Radio 4, 22 February 2007.
96. Joseph S. Nye Jr, 'Transformational Leadership and US Broad Strategy', *Foreign Affairs*, July/August 2006, p. 148.
97. Woodward, *State of Denial*, p. 241.
98. 'We did get the money to Iraq – dollars to dinars', *International Herald Tribune*, 27 February 2007.
99. Woodward, *State of Denial*, p. 82.
100. Ricks, *Fiasco*, p. 129.
101. *On the Ground*, Nicholas D. Kristof's *New York Times* blog.
102. Woodward, *Plan of Attack*, p. 249.
103. Ibid., George Tenet, 362
104. Lawrence Wilkerson, *PM*, BBC Radio 4, 11 May 2007.
105. George W Bush, *Decision Points*, p. 269.
106. Woodward, *State of Denial*, p. 249.
107. Ricks, *Fiasco*, p. 407.
108. Ibid., p. 408.
109. John Yoo, *War by Other Means: An Insider's Account of the War on Terror* (New York: Atlantic Monthly Press, 2006), p. 39.
110. Ibid., p. 43.
111. Brian Urquhart, 'The outlaw world', *New York Review of Books*, 11 May 2006.
112. Dick Cheney, *In My Time* (Threshold Editions, 2011), pp. 522–3.
113. http://www.bbc.co.uk/reithlectures
114. www.iraqinquiry.org.uk/media/40668/20091210amsawers-final.pdf
115. Tony Blair, *A Journey*, p. 452.
116. www.iraqinquiry.org.uk/media/40668/20091210amsawers-final.pdf
117. Ibid., 45534/100201-walker-final.pdf
118. Ibid., 51818/20110127-Boyce.pdf
119. Tony Blair, *A Journey* , pp. 464–5.
120. Sir Jeremy Greenstock, *Daily Telegraph*, 22 February 2007.
121. Liz Carpenter, *Ruffles and Flourishes: The Warm and Tender Story of a Simple Girl who Found Adventure in the White House* (Garden City, NY: Doubleday, 1970), p. 261.
122. Scott, *Tony & Cherie*, p. 227.
123. Review of Intelligence on Weapons of Mass Destruction, HC 898,14 July 2004.

124. Kevin Woods, James Lacey and Williamson Murray, 'Saddam's Delusions: The View from Inside', *Foreign Affairs*, May/June 2006, pp. 6–8.

125. Tenet, *At the Center of the Storm*, pp. 375–83.

126. Tom Bower, 'Blair's defence over Iraq is crumbling', *The Times*, 3 February 2007.

127. A very popular BBC tv satirical comedy first shown between 1980 and 1984. A sequel, *Yes, Prime Minister* ran from 1986 to 1988.

128. Labour's share of the popular vote was the lowest of any majority government in British history.

129. 'My Tony is fit . . . and up for it', *Sun*, 4 May 2005.

130. 'How not to run a country', interview with Lord Butler, *Spectator*, 9 December 2004.

131. 'The Secret World of Whitehall Part 2. Behind the Black Door', presented by Michael Cockerill, BBC 2.

132. General Sir Michael Rose, 'Enough of his excuses: Blair must be impeached over Iraq', *Guardian*, 10 January 2006.

133. David Owen, *Time To Declare: Second Innings* (London: Politico's, 2010), pp. 602–3.

134. Robert Rhodes James, *Gallipoli* (London: B. T. Batsford, 1965), pp. 350–1.

135. Hansard, HL Deb, 29 June 2006, vol. 683, col.1350.

136. Philip Ziegler, *Wilson: The Authorised Life of Lord Wilson of Rievaulx* (Weidenfeld & Nicolson, 1993), pp. 222–3.

137. Peter Oborne, 'Now Blair silences the Tories with his Euroscepticism. What a genius!', *Spectator*, 25 June 2005.

138. Richard Horton, 'A monstrous war crime', *Guardian*, 28 March 2007.

139. Roger Cohen, 'Why Iraq's resistance differs from insurgency', *International Herald Tribune*, 14–15 January 2006.

Susceptibility to hubris

1. Michael Scheuer, *Imperial Hubris: Why the West Is Losing the War on Terror* (Washington, DC: Potomac, 2005), p. 203.

2. Daniel Bell, *The Cultural Contradictions of Capitalism*, 20th anniversary ed. (New York: Basic, 1996), pp. 48–9.

3. Al Gore, speech, 23 September 2002.

4. Geoffrey Wheatcroft, 'The tragedy of Tony Blair', *Atlantic Monthly*, June 2004.

5. Tony Blair speaking to Steve Richards, chief political commentator for the *Independent* and presenter of GMTV's *Sunday* programme, October 2003.

6. Francis Beckett and David Hencke, *The Blairs and Their Court* (London: Aurum Press, 2004).

7. Dr Sarah Hale, *The Third Way and Beyond* (Manchester University Press, 2004).

8. Reinhold Niebuhr, *Moral Man and Immoral Society* (Charles Scribner's Sons, 1932, SCM Press, 1963), p.63.

9. David Hare, *Stuff Happens* (London: Faber & Faber, 2004), p. 10.

10. Norma Percy, 'An almighty splash', *Guardian*, 24 October 2005.

11. Geoffrey Perret, *Commander-in-Chief: How Truman, Johnson, and Bush Turned a Presidential Power into a Threat to America's Future* (New York: Farrar, Straus & Giroux, 2007), pp. 375 and 392.

12. Kevin Phillips, *American Theocracy: The Perils and Politics of Radical Religion, Oil, and Borrowed Money in the 21st Century* (New York: Viking Penguin, 2006), p. 99.

13. www.daedalustrust.org.uk

14. *Daily Mirror*, 27 October 2003.

15. 'Clinton reveals Blair heart scare details', *Independent*, 26 February 2004.

16. Peter Oborne, *The Rise of Political Lying* (London: Free Press, 2005), p. 97.

17. Interview with Jeremy Vine, BBC Radio 2.

18. David Blunkett, *The Blunkett Tapes: My Life in the Bear Pit* (London: Bloomsbury, 2006), p. 550.

19. *Evening Standard*, 20 November 2003. See also 3.45 p.m. lobby briefing by Prime Minister's official spokesman on the same day.

20. Paul Scott, *Tony & Cherie: A Special Relationship* (London: Sidgwick & Jackson, 2005), p. 219.

21. David Owen, 'Friendship, Adrenaline and Hubris', Institute of Neurology Annual Address and David Marsden Memorial Lecture, 5 October 2009. www.lorddavidowen.co.uk

22. Oborne, *Rise of Political Lying*, pp. 96 and 184.

23. Tony Blair, *A Journey* (London: Hutchinson, 2010), p. 510.

24. Kathleen T. Brady and Rajita Sinha, 'Co-Occuring Mental and Substance Use Disorders: The Neurobiological Effects of Chronic Stress', *American Journal of Psychiatry* (2005), vol. 162, pp. 1483–93.

25. Stanton Peele, 'Personality and Alcoholism: Establishing the Link', in David A. Ward (ed.), *Alcoholism: Introduction to Theory and Treatment*, 3rd ed. (Dubuque, IA: Kendall/Hunt, 1990), pp. 147–56.

26. John Heilemann, 'What's going on in George Bush's mind? A psychopolitical survey', *New York Magazine*, 5 February 2007.

27. Leo Abse, *Tony Blair: The Man behind the Smile* (London: Robson, 2001).

David Owen

28. Justin A. Frank, *Bush on the Couch: Inside the Mind of the US President* (London: Politico's, 2006), p. 202.

29. Nassir Ghaemi, *A First-Rate Madness: Uncovering the Links between Leadership and Mental Illness* (New York: Penguin Press, 2011).

30. Stephen Graubard, *The Presidents: The Transformation of the American Presidency from Theodore Roosevelt to George W. Bush* (London: Allen Lane, 2006), pp. 39 and 724.

31. Lord Morgan, 'The Judgement of History', *Parliamentary Monitor* (2007), vol. 149, pp. 16–17.

32. David Owen, 'Hubris and Nemesis in Heads of Government', *Journal of the Royal Society of Medicine* (2006), vol. 99, pp. 548–51; Simon Wessely, 'Commentary: The Psychiatry of Hubris', *Journal of the Royal Society of Medicine* (2006), vol. 99, pp. 552–3.

33. James Hillman, *The Force of Character: And the Lasting Life* (Ballantine, 1999), p. 178.

34. Nassir Ghaemi, *A First-Rate Madness: Uncovering the Links between Leadership and Mental Illness* (New York: Penguin Press, 2011), quoting from Tony Blair, *A Journey*, p.659.

Conclusions

1. House of Lords debate, 22 February 2007.

2. http://www.iraqinquiry.org.uk/media/52048/Laurie-2010-06-03-S1.pdf

3. Brian Jones, *Failing Intelligence* (London: Biteback, 2010), pp. 65–66. Brian Jones is the former head of the UK Defence Intelligence Staff's nuclear, biological and chemical section. His advice within government during the Iraq war was proven to have been correct and who appears, up to the time of writing, not to have been invited to give oral evidence to the Inquiry.

4. David Owen, *In Sickness and In Power* (London: Methuen, 2008), Chapter 3: 'Prime Minister Eden's illness and Suez'.

Index

Index

Index